THE PARISH

ALICE TAYLOR

LARGE PRINT
Oxford

First published in Great Britain 2008
by
Brandon
an imprint of Mount Eagle Publications

Published in Large Print 2011 by ISIS Publishing Ltd.,
7 Centremead, Osney Mead, Oxford OX2 0ES
by arrangement with
Brandon

British Library Cataloguing in Publication Data
Taylor, Alice, 1938–
    The parish.
    1. Village communities.
    2. Village communities - - Ireland.
    3. Sociology, Rural.
    4. Sociology, Rural - - Ireland.
    5. Large type books.
    I. Title
    307.7'2–dc22

ISBN 978–0–7531–5267–6 (hb)
ISBN 978–0–7531–5268–3 (pb)

Printed and bound in Great Britain by
T. J. International Ltd., Padstow, Cornwall

For Gabriel.
You were the wind beneath my wings.

Ar scáth a chéile a mhaireann na daoine.

Contents

Parish People

A parish is a tangle of all human life. Threads of tension and trust, kindness and begrudgery, generosity and meanness, harmony and jealousy, laughter and tears, all intermingle to create a patchwork of parish living. On marrying during the early 1960s into the village shop and post office, I became part of that patchwork. Parish-pump politics predominated and we all knew each other's business. Newcomers were scrutinised and researched and sometimes we found out more about them than they knew about themselves.

Some of the householders had farmyards behind their back doors where they kept poultry and pigs, and outside the village they had farms from which, morning and evening, the cows ambled into the backyards of the village to be milked. Farmers met daily at the local creamery, and after Sunday mass rows of men arranged themselves around the village corner to discuss parish affairs. A forge at the end of the village made shoes for donkeys, farm horses and racehorses; the harness maker looked after their working wear and their fancy Sunday harness. The blacksmith also made the bands for large timber wheels, put mend-its on metal pots and made the long-legged iron tongs for the open fire. On wet days and at night the forge became a social club where farmers met and exchanged farming and horse knowledge.

The local dressmaker catered for the ladies, and the tailor fitted out the men. Both of them turned and remodelled suits and coats, and many a good navy-blue serge got a second lease of life. Often grandfather's retired suit reappeared in the well-presented row of First Holy Communion attire. A carpentry shop was kept busy putting handles on pikes and shovels, repairing and making furniture, constructing coffins and the large timber wheels for farm carts. Young lads played hurling and football up and down the main street using their ganseys as goalposts, and in the event of a burst *sliotar* or football the local cobbler did the stitching. The barracks at the end of the street housed a sergeant and three gardaí at a time when the biggest offence in the parish was a bike without a light or a bull without a licence. The parish priest, wearing a long black skirt and a little bit of nonsense on his head, took care of other parish misdemeanours. His restrictive glance could sometimes be as effective as any garda baton.

There were four small shops in the village where people chatted across the high counters and kept up with the parish news; these shops catered for the entire needs of the parish from rosary beads to chamber pots. In them you could buy elastic for your knickers, corn plasters for aching feet, methylated spirits for the primus, Fynnon salts for lazy bowel movements and

Bob Martin's powders if your greyhound shared your problem. In them also all your grocery needs were met — even tea towels with a recipe for Gaelic Coffee. The know-how to make my first Gaelic Coffee was gleaned from one of these tea towels when a smart chef in Shannon Airport dreamed up this wonderful concoction to welcome travel-weary Americans and soothe their hearts with a warm Irish welcome.

We had four family-owned pubs from which the male regulars ran the world and sometimes went home only to turn. In one pub the woman of the house chopped her cabbage for the dinner on the counter as she doled out frothy pints. Cash-strapped customers would often instruct her to put their merry-making on the slate, and she was the mother confessor and counsellor to the distressed and inebriated.

Our shop, as part of the post office, manned the local telephone exchange. In there was an eight-day clock that Uncle Jacky, on the occasion of his marriage in 1932, had received from the local hurling and football club, and this provided a time check for the entire village. Children going to school put their heads in the door to see if they had a few spare minutes for the kick of a ball before school, and people on their way to mass or waiting for a funeral or bus checked the time on the post-office clock. The regulars who formed a perpetual guard of honour around the village corner could on request provide an instant and precise location for almost everyone in the parish. They observed who got on and off the bus and who walked and cycled through the village. They were the original community alert.

As part of the extended local telephone service we were supposed to know and keep the parish informed about the times of deaths, wakes and funerals. The farmers dropped in their AI calls for an Aberdeen Angus, Short-horn or Friesian and later these were collected by the man from the station, so we became familiar with the breeding patterns of the local cows. When the doctor or priest was missing, we took their calls, so we also knew who was arriving or departing from the parish. On arrival new babies were named after their grandparents, which could lead to a Johnny Jim Pat hanging off the family tree. The era of television names was yet to dawn. You were called after your ancestors and rooted into your own place. Crèches were unheard of and the extended family rocked the cradle. If the family name such as Murphy, O'Sullivan or McCarthy was too common in the parish, you had the Tommy Jim Pads and the Mary Jack Kates to distinguish between the different clans. Farmers had stay-at-home wives who double-jobbed between the house and the farmyard. They were the first working wives, who sold eggs weekly at the farm gate or to the village shop, and fattened geese and turkeys for the Christmas market.

You spun out your last days in your own home where you died in the comfort of your own bed. Many a man or woman was born and died in the same bed, four foot of black iron, bedecked with brass knobs top and bottom. No king or queen size, as the royals had not yet moved into the bedroom; all bedroom action was confined to four feet. Funeral parlours had yet to come in from America. The parlour was where you entertained visitors, and had nothing to do with your funeral. You certainly had no intention of being carted into one to lie in state when you were dead. Money was scarce and life was quite predictable and often boring.

Then the economy took off and the Celtic Tiger roared into the parish. He threw a switch that shot us all into fast-forward. Money poured into empty pockets. We wanted bigger and better houses. The tide of emigration turned and our young people were able to stay at home; as our economy soared, working Europe looked in our direction. They saw jobs and good wages. New houses were needed. Farming income alone slid down the financial ladder, so agricultural land became more valuable for building than for farming. Housing estates bearing titles with no connection to townland or landscape flooded out over green fields. People left the land, farm wives went out to work, and the farmyard became a silent place. For the first time, apartments replaced stables and cow houses on the rural landscape. As giant supermarket chains sprung up around the country, family businesses died in village and town centres.

Our parish, like many others, sprouted houses in remote corners. Young couples clipped heavy mortgages around their necks. Their parents might have been reared with a po under the bed but now their children had a bathroom at the end of every bed. Kitchens with state-of-the-art cooking facilities became the norm, but there was no time to cook. Stay-at-home mothers turned into working wives and needed cars. To reduce his stress, father took two holidays in the sun. There was no time to relax in his own home, but he bought another in foreign parts. The family car became a four-wheel-drive. Teenagers abandoned their bikes and became boy racers. Rural barracks closed and an automatic green plastic man on the barracks door replaced the local guard. Village homes became too valuable for living in and were turned into commercial units while the previous occupants built houses on approach roads. Thus we created the doughnut village. Traffic accelerated. Roads choked.

Today, we are all in the fast lane. No time for conversation. We exchange word bites: "too busy"; "no time". Two problems have sprouted. Who will hold the baby? Who will mind Nana? Life has turned into a marathon. We are all caught in the speed trap, but parish life still goes on. It moves around the church, the school, the parish hall and the GAA pitch. The church may not be as central to life as before but it is still needed for christenings, weddings and funerals. Some priests could be forgiven for thinking that they are now running a photography studio.

The school is vital for mushrooming parishes with young families. Putting on extensions requires huge local involvement. A mother who had previously been part of such an effort looked on one morning as still newer mothers lined up and was heard to comment caustically: "They are going in there now thinking that that school fell from the sky and they have no memory of the blood, sweat and tears that we put into getting all those extensions and facilities." A voluntary committee runs the parish hall; without it there would be no venue for indoor games and meetings, and as in every parish there are dozens of GAA stalwarts who put hours of unpaid effort into the young.

As parishes balloon, it requires a marriage of the new and the old to maintain community facilities. The newcomers and the parish permanents are slowly getting to know each other and finding out what makes the other tick. It is a challenging time. When a parish project needs attention, it's a case of "round up the usual suspects". Some deep-rooted parishioners believe in their divine right to do nothing. It would be easier to inject bounce into lead balls than get them to move. Some newcomers are reluctant to get involved and steer clear of anything that smacks of commitment. They consider themselves far too busy. But in both groups there are still enough movers and shakers who work to keep the show on the road.

Every parish has a story, and this is the story of our parish and our efforts to cope with the problems that are part of every parish in the first decade of the twenty-first century. We have the doers who get on with the job; the experts who feel too well informed to participate; the advisers whose function is to tell everyone how it should be done; and, of course, the hurlers on the ditch. But we are all part of the pot pourri that makes up life in the parish. We irritate each other, we help each other, we comfort each other and annoy the living daylights out of each other. But no matter how we all get along together, we still live in the shelter of each other.

CHAPTER ONE

Recording Roots

She beamed across the high counter of our village shop, her eyes dancing with anticipation, her face alive with excitement. In the subdued light of the small shop she glowed like an exotic poppy.

"My great great great great grandmother Kate Mullins was born here," she began breathlessly, and as I struggled to keep up with all the greats she continued in an excited American accent, "She left here after the famine."

Having sewn these seeds of information, she waited with wide-eyed expectation for her family tree to sprout up behind our counter. She was one of the hundreds of Americans who return each year to parishes all over Ireland to trace their roots.

"Do you know any more about her?" I prompted.

"That's about everything," she declared happily. "I'm just so delighted to have found her home place. I just knew that if I could find that, the rest would be easy," she confidently concluded. Joyful anticipation oozed from every pore. How could this vibrant positive girl be told that roots buried for over a hundred years did not sprout up on demand? They could require a lot of digging.

"Was it the parish or the village she came from?" I enquired tentatively, wanting to minimise the digging area.

"Oh!" she said in dismay, some of the delight draining from her face. "Is there a difference?"

"Well, it would help to limit possibilities," I assured her, feeling guilty to have to cast a cloud over her perfect happiness.

"But this is such a tiny place," she protested. "Everybody here must know everybody. This is Ireland!" She had obviously been reared on the American dream that Ireland was the promised land where she would be reconnected with her roots. In the face of her unbridled thirst for knowledge of her own people I felt a sense of responsibility. This girl was one of the descendants of the thousands of Irish who had been forced to emigrate and for years had sent home dollars that kept the roofs on family homes. Because I was reared in an old farmhouse where eight generations of the same family had lived, and from where many had been forced to emigrate, I had been taught that we owed them a huge debt of gratitude. My father, even if there was hay to be saved, had always taken time off from farming when the descendants of his ancestors came back to visit their home place.

At the other end of the counter Uncle Jacky, in a brown shop coat, was scooping sugar into paper bags and weighing it on the tall enamel scales where the wavering finger indicated when he had the bag full to its one-pound capacity. His roots went as far back as hers into the soil of Innishannon. Though he had overheard our conversation he had left me to my own resources. I was new to the village shop, having only recently married his nephew Gabriel, and Uncle Jacky was probably letting me find out that there was more to running a village shop than just selling bread and jam. Now he walked over to us, easing his glasses to the top of his head, and stood thinking for a few minutes. With a face glowing with expectation, the American watched hopefully, waiting for him to pull the story of Kate Mullins out of his pocket. Uncle Jacky scratched his head, wrinkling up his face in deep concentration. This was going to take time. After all, we were travelling back over a hundred years. The young American struggled hard to keep silent.

"Mullins is not a local name," he said thoughtfully, and the light waned in the vivacious face, but rose again as he continued: "though I think that I remember an old woman saying that there were Mullinses here a long time ago."

"Oh, how wonderful!" she breathed, her face alight with delight.

"They could have lived up in Rathnaroughy."

There was an impressed silence from the American and then, with a look of dazed pleasure on her face, she whispered, "Say that again and say it very, very slowly. I have never heard of such a beautiful-sounding place."

"Now, I could be wrong," Uncle Jacky said quickly before she got carried away by the sound of Rathnaroughy, but there was no holding this girl back.

"Rough . . . raw . . . rugby," she drawled in ecstasy and Uncle Jacky winced in pain at the verbal assassination of this ancient Gaelic townland.

"The best thing to do now, girleen," he advised her confidentially across the counter, "is to go down the village to the carpenter's shop at the end of the street and the man there might be able to do a bit better than myself."

"You're a great guy," she assured him, and, with a melting look that would have given a younger man bad thoughts, headed for the door, calling over her shoulder, "I'll be right back!"

"Were you trying to get rid of her?" I asked Uncle Jacky in surprise because that would not be his style.

"No, no," he assured me convincingly. "Jeremiah goes back much further than myself and if there was ever Mullinses here he's her best chance. Then we'll send her to Billy in the forge and between the three of us we'll surely dig up something."

He was right, and by evening, after much to and froing and joint consultations across our counter, and further inquiries, they had dug deeply and found a trail that had traced the story of Kate Mullins back to an old stone house at the other end of the street. It had taken up a lot of their time but for that day tracing the roots of this young American was their first priority. Billy had horses to be shod, Jeremiah had doors to be made, and Jacky had customers to be served, but all this could be intermingled through their genealogical research. Their commitment to helping this young American was impressive and it was easy to see that they felt duty bound to assist her in finding her roots. They did not articulate it but it was obvious to me that their generation, like my father, felt a responsibility to the children of those who had been forced to emigrate. Because they themselves had been able to remain at home they felt that they had a duty to keep the home fires burning for those who had been forced to leave.

Over the following years, Jacky, Jeremiah and Billy helped many visitors to trace their ancestors. It was interesting to see how from very few seeds they could trace a whole family tree. The key to their success was their knowledge of their own place and their interest in and love of its people. In their desire to help they often called in others and sometimes the weaving of the full story involved a dozen or more people. Jeremiah Mawe was the oldest and the most knowledgeable and the day he died he took a big slice of our local history with him. For many years after his death, people were heard to comment "Jeremiah would have known that". Then in 1977 Uncle Jacky died and the same thing applied. Soon the entire social history of our parish would be buried in the graveyard. Something needed to be done or our knowledge and sense of pride in our own place would disappear. The roots of any parish are necessary for the healthy well-being of its future. Like trees we need to be rooted in some corner of the universe; otherwise, when the storms of life erupt, we could be blown away.

In the early 1980s we held a history exhibition in the dressing rooms of the local hurling and football club. The aim of the exercise was to gather together all the folklore and history of the parish. We invited people to submit anything that they thought might be of parish interest, be it a story, poem or picture, and we asked the children to talk to their grandparents and write up the family history. The resulting collection was displayed in the dressing rooms and viewed with great interest by the people of the parish. Old family photographs, maps and family histories were on display, and a beautiful oil painting of the derelict houses at the eastern end of the village. Most of us up to then had regarded these old houses as an eyesore, but now we saw them through the eyes of artist Lia Walsh. It was the first time that many of us had seen Lia's work as she had only just come to live in the parish, but as a result of the response to that picture she set up our first art class and for many of us opened the door into the world of painting. It is this interlinking of people's skills that forms the basis for a parish community.

At that history exhibition, the item that caused most interest was a detailed history of the village, written by Peg Santry. Peg had been a teenager working in one of the big houses outside the village when "the troubles", as we call them, broke out. She was of a Catholic republican family but had an understanding and fondness for her Protestant Anglo-Irish employer and, like many others at the time, was caught on the horns of a dilemma. For this reason she was able to tell both sides of the story. She also knew everybody in the parish and, beginning with the first house at the top of the street, she wrote about each family in great detail.

Most people when asked to write an article view it as a major undertaking, but Peg just put pen to paper and spilled out her story, which she called "My Innishannon Long Ago". She began with the words of Katherine Tynan Hinkson's poem, "The Wind that Shakes the Barley":

There's music in my heart all day,
I hear it late and early.
It comes from fields far far away
The wind that shakes the barley.

Peg was a natural storyteller and people were fascinated by what she had written. We had only one copy of everything on display, including Peg's story, and people had to queue up to read it. After each reading, long discussions took place. As we watched this happen, the germ of an idea took root. A magazine could be written by the people of the parish to record the past and present. Like many other parishes, ours is an old and historic place and every senior citizen who died was taking a little bit of the living history of the parish with them. We decided to have our own Christmas magazine; it would be called *Candlelight*.

It was 1983 and we had never heard of desk-top publishing; computers were only for the chosen few. We did not have a bull's notion about how to compile or publish a magazine, but we had a lot of enthusiasm, even though it was thickly laced with ignorance!

The following February, we went around and asked people to write. The immediate response was "What

15

will I write about?" and the answer was always the same: "Feel free." We wanted a magazine that would reflect all the different facets of the parish. Contributors were told that they had several months in which to write their articles. That was mistake number one! If people feel that they have plenty of time, they put things off.

One of the people we were most anxious to have on board was Jer, who was known in the parish as "the Twin", and who over the years had thought up witty and entertaining poems about parish events. None of these were written down, but they were floating around at the back of the Twin's head.

On the day of the Twin's eightieth birthday, I met him in our shop.

"How are you?" I inquired.

"I'm good," he told me enthusiastically. "And when you are good, you should say that you are good."

"Any particular reason?" I asked.

"I've met an old girlfriend," he said with a smile. "And tonight we're going for a drink."

"Well, isn't that great," I declared.

"There's only one thing bothering me," he said seriously.

"What's that?"

"I wouldn't want her now to think that this would go any further."

At a time when most people of his age are busy counting their pills and watching their blood pressure, here was the Twin at eighty occupied with the possibility that an old girlfriend might lose the run of herself. He had never married, and his long life was full of romantic interludes, which he often recorded in verse. He remembered one particular girlfriend in song.

In six months' long courting she never came late
But right on the dot she was out at the gate.
And my Mary would often point out the old site
Where O'Neill and O'Donnell were beat in the fight.
But 'twasn't long after that we too were at war
When she asked me politely to teach her the car.
To explain the position I really am bound
To say not an apt pupil in Mary I found.
Sure to sit and look on it would bring you to tears
As she burnt with the clutch and tore with the gears,
But I had no patience and she had great skill
I was told by the lassie from the top of Sand Hill.
Now we had many bumps and we had many spills
But we ne'er had a tiff till down by Jagoe's Mills
We were going for the ditch when I gave a wee shout
And I knew by her face that 'twas all up the spout.
She told me of driving she now had her fill
And to take her right home to the top of Sand Hill.
When she told me she never would drive it again
Those words surely shook the poor heart of the Twin.

The Twin was interested in the whole *Candlelight* enterprise, and for that year and every year until he died he pulled a poem from the back of his archival mind.

In many parishes there are people like the Twin who are fascinated by the stories of their own place and

17

people and have the gift of putting them together in entertaining poems and stories. It is regrettable that sometimes their stories die with them.

In 1984, a parish magazine constituted a new venture and people were a bit apprehensive and loath to put pen to paper. So, with the deadline looming, I decided to write a few articles to have them in reserve to act as fillers if necessary. They were never needed because slowly articles began to come in from around the parish and some from further afield. We had contacted people who had left the parish, and some — including Con Murphy of GAA fame, who never forgot his roots — came good.

For that first edition most features came in handwritten, and Maureen, assisted by Mary, took on the task of typing them up. The next step was to get a cover, and here we were blessed with the genius of young Denis who lived up Bóthar na Sop and was studying architecture. He designed a classic cover with a perfect drawing of our village lit by a giant candle and guarded by flying cherubs. It was the ideal Christmas cover and perfectly suited to the name *Candlelight*. On the back cover we put an old photograph, from the Lawrence collection, of the western end of the village in the 1890s, a view which had, by 1984, almost totally changed. We found that all the expertise we required existed within the parish, and indeed this expertise can probably be found in most places.

On the first page, to capture the whole essence of the *Candlelight* concept, we put a photograph of a little girl in a long nightdress, lighting a Christmas candle. Every year afterwards we added another child, and now we have twenty-four children, alternating each year between boys and girls. After the first ten years we had the challenging scenario of trying to have ten children simultaneously looking angelic and lighting ten candles without at the same time setting fire to the candle-lighter in front of them. After a few close shaves, with singed hair and scorched fingers, we decided on a cutoff point of five children. The earlier photographs were then transferred to the sides of the page and framed the new children in the centre. Over the years we discovered the main qualification for a *Candlelight* child was to have a pleasant and helpful mother!

So, after a certain amount of huffing and puffing, the first *Candlelight* saw the light of day. We were a printer's nightmare because we hadn't a clue. However, whereas in some cases I might be a slow learner, where *Candlelight* was concerned there was no time for pussy-footing about, so I learned fast. We sold it in our own parish, in Kinsale and Bandon, and we lost money. The point of the exercise was never about making money but we still needed to get our financial act together. The following year we got sponsorship from a few well-to-do professionals in the parish, and there are generous people like that in every parish but you cannot keep going back to them indefinitely, so the following year we charged enough to cover our expenses. Finally we got a proper grip on the situation and decided that, if we believed in the *Candlelight* concept, we would need to set a decent price and any profit would go to parish projects.

To date we have restored a huge historic parish map of the village which is in the local church and we have helped finance a village sculpture of Billy the Blacksmith. *Candlelight* is written by the people of the parish, so any returns belong to the parish. It is probably something that is happening in many other parishes up and down the country.

We may have originally considered *Candlelight* a once-off, but as soon as the first edition hit the parish, people started to talk about the following year. It soon dawned on us that it was now expected to be a permanent feature of the parish Christmas. One man who had previously refused to write because he deemed it to be beyond him said to me, "Well, was that all ye wanted?" and so decided to do an article.

Over the twenty-four years, *Candlelight* has served many purposes. After the first edition, one woman told us, "You know something: that Christmas magazine has somehow brought us all together under the one umbrella." She had a very good point as it keeps those of us within the parish aware of what is going on because everyone is free to write and tell their own story, and it keeps people long gone from the parish in touch with their home place.

The real treasures are the old school photographs; people are fascinated by them. Sometimes there might be only one such photograph in the parish, and when we publish it everyone enjoys a trip down memory lane. From the Twin we got one of these photos that had been taken about sixty years earlier, and not only did we get the photograph but we also got a detailed description of the day it was taken. Apparently that morning before going to school the Twin, who always possessed a sense of occasion, had wanted to put on his good suit for the photo call but his mother would not allow him. "And there now," he proclaimed six decades later, "wasn't she wrong because I'd be looking much better now in my new suit."

The photograph, like all black and white photographs of the time, was crystal clear, but it was unframed and the folder holding it a bit battered around the edges. After that Christmas we had the photograph framed to preserve it for the Twin, who hung it up in his front hall where it was admired by all his callers. After he died, I went to his auction to buy the photograph for the local school. It was in a box with other odds and ends and I took note of the number. However, just before it came under the hammer, I went back to check on the box, only to discover that the photograph was gone. Somebody had taken it. It takes all kinds of people to make up a parish!

Candlelight records things that would otherwise be lost and often, when a contributor dies, their family is glad to have their *Candlelight* articles, some written many years previously. New families are now coming to live around the parish and *Candlelight* fills them in on the history of their chosen place. It also gives new writing talent a sounding platform; one of our original writers is now with *The Irish Times* and another with the *Irish Examiner*. We are not claiming that we contributed in any way to their success, but it makes us feel good to think that they started with us.

Some of our writers now have their names written in the golden book and to browse though the back numbers is to realise how much our parish has changed over the last twenty-four years. The cow shed that was behind Jeremiah's carpenter shop is now the Private Collector Art Gallery, selling original Irish art at prices that in Jeremiah's time could have bought out the entire village.

Over those years, some writers came to us from the most unexpected places. Having read my book, *The Village*, one man wrote to me from England. His mother had been one of the travelling people and she had called to all the houses on the road from Innishannon to Kinsale. Later he was taken into care as his father had got into difficulties, and the young lad spent his childhood in the orphanage of St Patrick's Upton in our parish. At the age of sixteen, he went to work with a local farmer and one night, coming home from a fair in Bandon, the farmer and himself had visited Mrs Hawkins behind her butcher's shop in our village. There, he wrote, he got the biggest and the first steak that he had ever seen. He went on to tell how he had left Ireland and gone to work down the coalmines in England. There was a scheme prevailing at the time whereby your fare was paid and in return you went to work down the mines. When he got out of the coalmines, he became a long-distance lorry driver and did well.

His letter was articulate and well written, with no trace of bitterness. He had experienced a life style that very few had documented and I knew from his letter that he could write a good article. The following summer he came back to Ireland and called to see me. He was a grand man and, after a short time in his company, I felt that the world was a better place. He had a lady wife now and two attractive daughters, but he talked about his time in the orphanage and how good they were to him, adding, "The food was bad but they had no better themselves." He also told me about walking down to the village to see the travelling theatre groups known as the fit-ups.

I gave him a copy of *Candlelight*, suggesting that he might like to write his story, and sure enough, we published it the following Christmas. Shortly afterwards he wrote to tell me that he had been diagnosed with terminal cancer and that his time would be short. In life he had got off to a tough start but he had pulled himself up by his bootlaces and carved out a good quality of life for himself and his family. He was one of the most positive and well-rounded people that I had ever met and I was glad that he had written his story for *Candlelight*. Great people like him should not leave life without getting the opportunity to tell their story, and sometimes their story helps to keep others afloat.

CHAPTER
TWO

A Step in Time

"Have you thought about the millennium?" asked a tentative voice at the other end of the phone.

"Well, not really," I said, taken by surprise. "Sure, that's months away."

"People are already planning what they're going to do," she told me.

"Don't I know it?" I assured her. "They seem to be flying in all directions for the occasion."

"Do you think that we should have something in the parish hall?" she asked

"Will there be anyone left in the parish to go to it?" I wondered.

"At the moment it looks doubtful, but the very young and the old won't be going anywhere, and wouldn't it be nice to have something for them?"

"I suppose it would," I agreed. "Did you have anything in mind?"

"Well, nothing in particular," she said vaguely, "but I thought that we might organise something. You're good at that kind of thing." As alarm bells began to ring in my head, she continued: "That 'Meet the Neighbours' night was a great success and wouldn't something like that be grand?"

A few years previously a "Meet the Neighbours" night had been organised for the newcomers to the parish so that they could get to know each other and meet the home-grown residents. The night could hardly be described as having achieved the purpose for which it was intended because most of the newcomers never came, but for those who did, it had been a great night. Our village, like many other small villages, was expanding at such a rate that we could lose our sense of being a village, and nights that brought us together helped us to retain that sense.

After the phone call I sat at the kitchen table and wondered where to begin or whether to begin at all. Diarmuid, who was in his twenties, breezed in and sized me up pretty quickly.

"You look a bit bothered," he declared, viewing me across the table.

I filled him in on the phone call and he grinned, rubbing his hands together.

"Mother," he gleefully informed me, "you've got a jumping monkey."

"What's that?" I demanded.

"Well, in our business if you have a job that you want to get done but don't want to do yourself, then you have a jumping monkey. So the trick is to meet up with a colleague and pass on the job. Then the jumping monkey jumps from your back on to their back. So, Mother, a jumping monkey has just landed on your back!"

"If I decide to hold on to him, do you think that people would come to the parish hall on the night of the millennium?" I asked.

"Not a hope in hell," he told me. "Sure, wouldn't it be full of screeching children and old fogies?"

"Like me," I said.

During that day I ran the idea past some people in our shop. The village shop and post office is a great place to be if you want to do a parish survey on anything. But the general reaction to the millennium night was that nobody with a glint of imagination or a sense of adventure would be found in the parish hall on the night. Faraway places beckoned. That evening I put the idea to my husband Gabriel who always had his finger on the pulse of the parish.

"Well, of course we should have something in the hall," he declared. "When millennium night comes around, a lot of those high flyers will have come down to earth."

Later, when our cousin Con, who had been part of the family for over thirty years, came home from his school in Bandon with a bundle of textbooks under his arm, I asked: "Con, what had you planned to do for the millennium?"

"Never even gave it a thought," he told me mildly.

That was the end of my survey and, as with lots of surveys, I was as wise at the end as I had been at the beginning.

The following week a supplement fell out of a newspaper that I was reading on a train home from Dublin. The headline ran "Last Light Ceremony". I read and reread the article, marvelling at the simplicity and imagination of the entire concept. The idea was that everyone in Ireland was to be furnished with a millennium candle to be lit on the evening of the old millennium so that the entire country could be united in this Last Light ceremony. The accompanying message with the candle would read: "As the sun sets on the millennium on December 31st 1999, the National Millennium Committee invites you to join with family and friends, neighbours or colleagues, to light your millennium candle at this milestone in history. *Mílaois faoi sheán is faoi mhaise.*"

It was, I thought, an imaginative and visionary concept. The last light of the millennium would fade out over Dursey Sound and our parish would be in its dying rays. Our parish could build its whole millennium celebration, incorporating the congregations of both churches, around the Last Light ceremony. We would gather in Christ Church at four o'clock, which was the scheduled time for the Last Light ceremony, and later go up the hill to St Mary's for a second ceremony, and finish with a party in the parish hall to welcome in the new millennium. The possibilities of the project gave me food for thought that lasted the entire train journey.

When I got home, I rang my friend Joy, an active member of the Church of Ireland.

"Joy, what do you think of a Last Light ceremony in Christ Church at four o'clock for both congregations and later a joint ceremony in our church and then a party in the parish hall for all of us?"

"Sounds great," she enthused. "But will all of you come to our church?"

"Of course we'll come," I assured her, never doubting it for a moment. Relations between both congregations had always been cordial; we attended each other's weddings and funerals, though up to this we had never shared ceremonies. We ran the idea past both sets of clergy and there was no problem.

That year, Christmas took a back seat as the whole country waited with bated breath for the coming of the new millennium. It seemed that people were planning to be in the most exotic of places to welcome it in.

On Christmas Eve, a man from the bogs of North Cork came into our village selling huge pieces of bog deal. He was pointed in my direction and his cargo made me gasp in awe. What would be more appropriate as a centre-piece for a millennium celebration than bog deal from the deep belly of ancient Ireland? This bog deal was probably as old as the millennium itself. There was a huge claw-like *creachaill* on the top of the trailer which was the jewel in the crown of the load. It was probably placed there to act as bait. He was a large, jovial man in a hand-knitted jumper, with a twinkle in his eye, and would have made a great Santa Claus. But this was no Santa Claus! He had what I wanted and he knew it. Like the cattle jobbers at the fairs of old I tried to mask my enthusiasm, and so began a long bargaining session.

He assured me regularly: "Ah, Missus, you'll never see the likes of it again!" He was right, but I sensed that he had raised his prices to an exorbitant level in order to bring them down and make me feel that I was getting a bargain. It rained softly down on us and his knitted gansey draped across his large round belly glistened with raindrops, but we were both so stuck into our wrangling that we would not give in to the rain or to each other.

Eventually we reached a compromise, but to get a good price I had to take the entire load, so he probably came out the better of the deal. But I had enjoyed battling wits with him and he told me, "You're a hard woman, but sure 'twas great doing business with you and I wouldn't have enjoyed it half as much if you gave in on the first round."

So he stacked the bog deal in the backyard and every day I admired it and loved it more. I recalled the *creachaill*s of bog deal that had been brought home from the bog when I was a child. We had splintered them up to start the fire and my father had used them to light his pipe. Sometimes they were pared into long strips to act as scallops for thatching. Now they are no longer needed for practical purposes but they speak to us of an earlier age when they formed the floor of an ancient Ireland. It was wonderful to have this treasury of the past to welcome in the new millennium.

During the days of the dying year, a small group of us moved into both churches. Old candelabras that had been relegated to the lower regions of Christ Church and into the abandoned gallery of St Mary's were polished and brought back into active service. Candles and flowers were the order of the day in both churches but for the parish hall a more flamboyant atmosphere

29

was required for the parish party. The dark red curtains of the stage became the backdrop for two enormous silver trees, festooned with blue stars, and Elizabeth brought in her solid silver candelabra with blue candles for centre-stage. In every parish there are big-hearted people like Elizabeth, blessed with a great sense of occasion.

The balcony at the back of the hall was smothered by Noreen in mounds of ivy, threaded through with silver ribbons. Our best flower arranger, Rose, created a huge arrangement in the millennium colours of blue and silver, and the food tables around the hall were draped in white and silver cloths. We had bought wine and soft drinks and the parishioners brought in an abundance of home-made food.

The women of parishes around Ireland will still come good when it comes to providing eats for festive occasions, and fortunately we have not yet reached the stage where we need to get in professional caterers to provide for parish events. There is a great sense of togetherness in the sharing of bread that has been baked by parish people. As I watched the laden trays arrive, I felt that a large communal cake had been baked and would later be shared by all. By late afternoon, we were ready to feed a small army, though we still had no idea of numbers.

To welcome in a new year, not to mention a millennium, a clock was needed to add a sense of drama to the occasion. We required a substantial timepiece, preferably a grandfather. But could you ask anyone to move a valuable grandfather clock and bring it to the parish hall? We did not need to ask because one farming couple, Ted and Phil, not only offered their clock but Ted brought it along in his tractor and trailer. We all held our breath, wondering how grandfather would take to his new position in front of the stage, but once he was level, he took the move like a man, and tick-tocked into action. In the centre of the hall we had laid out the huge sea of ancient bog deal and on it we mounted an enormous millennium candle. It was an island of bog deal and light, around which the activity would flow. All was ready for the party to begin!

It was a calm misty evening as we climbed the steps of Christ Church, and the trees in Dromkeen Wood across the river were slowly gathering their dusky coats around them. Along the street the shadows were drifting into doorways and silently people were emerging and all heading in the one direction. The traffic on the road outside had slowed to almost non-existent as by now everyone in the whole country had gone to their chosen places to welcome in the millennium. People were pouring into Christ Church and taking time to sign the leather-bound Millennium Book, which would be a record of all those present on this historic night. The seating capacity of Christ Church is about three hundred and fifty, and every seat was occupied, and more people were standing along by the walls. Joy and her friends were trying to find a place for everybody and eventually there were almost five hundred people packed into the church.

When the incoming tide waned, it was decided that the ceremony should begin. A delighted Canon

31

Burrows — who was later to become Archbishop of Cashel — emerged from the vestry and assured us smilingly that he was not accustomed to such a packed house. He rose to the occasion with an inspiring homily befitting a special event, which he combined with playing the organ and leading the people in songs of praise.

Some lights had been left on to guide people to their seats and now these were all turned off. The church was in darkness. Slowly three members of St Mary's emerged from the back porch and walked up the aisle, bearing the gift of a tall Jubilee candle which they placed on a central table. Canon Burrows lit it from a little candle that he had brought from Iona earlier that year. St Columcille had taken the light of Christianity from Ireland to Iona in the sixth century, and this gave the small candle a special symbolism. A light was then carried to the candles in the windows, and the light slowly spread along the pews as all the little millennium candles were lit. This was the idea of the National Millennium Committee becoming a reality: the church was aglow with candlelight, and voices were raised in songs of praise as we all sang from the same hymn sheet.

Afterwards people drifted slowly from the church, reluctant to leave the communal pool of peace. Some stayed on to sign the Millennium Book which had not been possible for all on the way in, and as they queued now, they chatted quietly. The Jubilee candle was left lighting in the centre of the church, and on the gothic windowsills candle-lit floral arrangements flickered light along the now empty pews. As we went down the sloping pathway from the church, we looked back at the candles softly illuminating the rich stained-glass windows.

Then three members of Christ Church brought the still-lighting Jubilee candle through the village and up the hill to St Mary's. Our parish priest welcomed them and led them in procession to the altar. Twenty-four people followed the candle-bearers, all members of different parish organisations, each carrying a symbol of their own organisation. On the steps of the altar, six people represented the different age groups in the parish, ranging from Denis, the oldest at eighty-seven, to Sarah Louise, the youngest at four months. The light was passed down through the ages and then down along the church. The small millennium candles glowed for the second time that night and the dark church was turned into a sea of wavering candles. Members of both churches did the readings and raised their voices in songs of united praise.

Afterwards the Jubilee candle led a candlelight procession down the hill and along the village street to the parish hall. With the street empty of traffic, it was a night when our parish could move at its own pace.

The parish hall was transformed into a wonderland. The beautiful grandfather clock in front of the stage looked down over lit candelabras on tables of food and wine. The huge candle in the centre of the sea of bog deal was lit, and slowly the hall filled to overflowing, and we wined and dined, keeping an eye on the clock.

33

Long-separated friends were reunited with whoops of joy and delighted hugs. In the excitement of the reunion, full glasses of wine were abandoned. Later, when the owners went to recover their glasses, faces took on baffled expressions. Locals who had wisely held on to their drinks smiled knowingly and quietly refilled the empties. Old Johnny with the big thirst had unobtrusively slipped around, tossing back unguarded glasses. Never before had he got such a free supply — all his Christmases had come together! (The following day, he was so sick from over-indulgence that he turned over a new leaf and became a teetotaller. Miracles are not always as a result of divine intervention.)

One strikingly handsome young man home for the occasion flitted like a butterfly around all the pretty girls. He worked the room like a politician before an election. My friend Joan, who likes to call a spade a spade, viewed him with a jaundiced eye. She was well versed in his colourful curriculum vitae. When he began to chat up her daughter and mine, she strode purposefully across the hall to me, and with the look of a high court judge on her face, she pronounced acidly: "The two of us would want to keep an eye on that fella. Given half a chance he could make grandmothers out of the two of us."

Slowly the long, golden hand of grandfather climbed upwards, and, as it neared twelve, we all gathered in a circle. The countdown began. Suddenly the time was upon us and we were welcoming in the millennium with hugs, tears and kisses. Then the doors of the hall were thrown open and the bells of both churches pealed in the millennium as grandfather finished striking twelve.

When the bells finished pealing, the soft background music in the hall changed tempo and people decided that it was time to dance. And so the hours were danced away and photographs were taken. It was a night to be held in cameo. When we finally left the parish hall in the early hours of the new millennium, we knew that this night of light would be forever imprinted on the back pages of our minds. The idea of the National Millennium Committee to give each of us a millennium candle had illuminated the whole occasion. This special night had been celebrated all over the world but in Ireland the Last Light ceremony had given the Irish celebration a special sense of togetherness. We had been united by light.

CHAPTER
THREE

The Beekeeper

The Christmas of the millennium year brought to an abrupt end a story that had been interwoven through our lives for many years but to tell that story we must go back to the day it began.

It was the late summer of 1968 and as I walked along the corridor that led from the kitchen to the front hallway of our guesthouse, situated at the village corner, I wondered about the cousin who my husband Gabriel had told me was looking for accommodation. As I came into the front hall, a pale-faced, dark-haired young man smiled uncertainly at me. There was about him an aura of tranquillity.

"Our cousin Maura told me to call to you," he said quietly. "I'm coming to teach in Bandon and would like to stay until I find some place there."

"Well, we are really only open during the summer months for the tourists," I told him, "but you're welcome to stay for a week until you find a place in Bandon."

"A week will be fine," he said with a smile.

So Con came into our lives. He came for a week and stayed for over thirty years. At the time, we had three young teachers from local schools staying with us, along with my sister; they had been sharing our home for a few years and had become part of the kitchen scene, together with my husband Gabriel and our three small boys, aged six, three and one. Con fitted in like a bird into a nest. He had come from a household with five brothers and no sisters, but now he was surrounded by five women and became the adopted brother in his new family. He was quiet, gentle and considerate, and if we had gone out and looked for somebody to be part of our household, we could not have found anybody more suitable.

For Gabriel he was somebody who shared his great love of sports, and they spent many hours discussing matches. The two of them shared a deep affection for the Irish language and culture, and they started Irish nights — *Oíche Ghaeilge* — in the parish hall and tried to turn us all into fluent Irish speakers and top-class Irish dancers. They may not have succeeded 100 per cent but we had great fun practising the intricacies of a two-hand reel and weaving our way through the haymaker's jig.

One of our neighbours, Kathleen, who lived across the road, later told me that those nights had given her a deep appreciation of the Irish language and culture. Con, who taught Maths and Science in nearby St Brogan's, gave grinds to children from all over the parish simply because he could never say no to a distressed mother; he always assured a parent who worried that they did not have a bright spark on their hands that most education was 99 per cent perspiration and 1 per cent inspiration.

To Aunty Peg and Uncle Jacky, who lived next door, he became a regular caller, brightening up their lives, and Aunty Peg and himself often enjoyed a quiet drink together in her little sitting room behind the shop. If their beloved Gabriel had to be away, they felt that we were all in safe hands while Con was around. As a child, I had lost a much-loved brother called Connie, and for years had silently mourned his loss, and now this blessing of another Con had come into my life and taken his place.

One sunny summer's day a swarm of bees found its way into Jacky's garden much to the consternation of all. The bees hung off the branch of a tree in the middle of the garden and we all admired them from a safe distance. Aunty Peg decided that it would be very unlucky to let them go because she believed that if bees came, you looked after them; otherwise they went and took your good luck with them. That was fine in theory but the practical reality of non-beekeepers handling a swarm of bees was another thing altogether. A bucket and a sheet were brought into the garden, and because Aunty Peg believed that you rang a bell to keep a swarm from flying away, a bell clanged in the background.

Gabriel and Con approached the tree, one holding the bucket and the other with a stout stick with which to hit the branch and cause the bees to fall into the bucket that was to be promptly covered with the sheet. That was the plan, but the bees had other ideas! As the two prospective beekeepers cautiously approached the tree, Aunty Peg continued to ring the bell and we all stood well back, shouting words of encouragement and caution. We were enough to drive any swarm into a demented state, which was exactly what happened. When the branch got a severe thump, some of the swarm fell into the bucket but the remainder went into a frenzied buzzing attack on the two beekeepers, who dropped the bucket and ran for their lives with angry bees in hot pursuit. The rest of us dived for cover all over the garden. The bees won that battle and within minutes had the place to themselves.

However, as the day passed, they swarmed around the bucket, and under the calming influence of approaching darkness it was then possible to cover them cautiously with Aunty Peg's sheet. I doubted her belief in the bell-ringing theory, but wrong or right we now had a swarm of bees. A hive was procured from my brother who was a beekeeper in North Cork, and so Con and Gabriel became beekeepers in the back garden and the hives gradually increased over the years. Gabriel, because of his long hours in the shop and post office as well as being involved in every organisation in the parish, was often short of beekeeping time but Con's job, with its long holidays, lent itself to beekeeping. He was the ideal beekeeper, patient and painstaking, with an infinitely inquiring mind that became completely fascinated by the bees.

At the top of our garden stands an old stone, ivy-covered building that we call the Old Hall because it was once a Methodist preaching hall. It faces south, and in front of it is a raised pathway cushioned by years of falling leaves. Along this pathway Con's hives stood in a row. The first tree I planted in the garden was a lime because a lime tree provides as rich a harvest for the bees as an acre of clover. It was a totally impractical step because a lime tree is far too big for an ordinary-sized garden and now it acts as an umbrella for a large portion of the lawn. The day I planted that little tree I sat beside it and wrote a poem.

The Honey Tree
The day was soft and mellow,
Growth was in the ground;
I went into the garden,
Climbed to the honey sound,
Eased my spade through the fallen leaves
Of golden brown and red
And as I lifted out the earth
I made a soft brown bed.
Mother nature opened wide
Her arms of velvet brown
And on her maternal lap
I laid my young tree down.
All around the soft young roots
I folded mother earth
And when my baby tree stood tall
I felt joy as in a birth.
I tied her to a firm stake
To hold her in the sways,
A seasoned piece of older wood
To guard her growing days.

Con became a dedicated beekeeper, and some summers Gabriel and himself went off to Gormanstown to take beekeeping courses; Con spent much of his long holidays caring for the bees and making hives. He passed many contented hours at the top of the garden, his white-suited figure moving quietly between the hives. When they swarmed, the bees usually hung off the same branch in the garden and then we circled around them, but gone were the days of bell-ringing and mayhem. A swarm of bees hanging off a branch is a fascinating sight, and often customers from the shop came into the garden to admire them.

When I became a gardener, the bees and I often had a running battle which they always won because their ammunition was a good deal sharper than anything I could muster. On a fine day, when they were busy collecting honey, there was no way they were going to allow me to weed around their territory. I was an obstacle that had to be moved, and often I had to make a hasty run for the back door, but sometimes they got me before I made my escape. Con was always amused by their persistence in getting rid of me and advised waiting until late evening to weed around them. But I was always prepared to take a chance and often paid the price for my obstinacy with a few painful stings. Con would smile and say, "You can't get the better of the bees."

Extracting time was Con's harvest and he gloried in the different kinds of honey: the clover honey and the hawthorn honey and the different taste of each. He would hold the jars up to the light of the window the better to savour their colour and texture, and when we stored them in a deep cupboard they glowed with a rich golden warmth.

Stored Summer
Bridal hedges of whitethorn
Cascade on to green fields;
Under bulging wings
The gliding bees
Collect their nectar,
Bearing it back
To humming hives.
Extraction time,
The pregnant combs
Release their ripened treasure,
Pouring golden liquid
Into sparkling jars.
In a deep cupboard
Spirit of warm days
Bring to barren winter
The taste of whitethorn honey.

We sold some of the honey in the shop and once people got the taste of it, demand exceeded supply and so we took bookings for "Con's Honey", which was usually sold out in advance of extraction.

One of the by-products of honey is wax and, when this had accumulated into vast amounts, we decided one Christmas that we would make wax candles. First, the wax had to be melted down, which Con did in a special tray over the Aga. It was a messy, smelly job but resulted in round slabs of yellow wax that gave off the beautiful rich smell of honey. Then began the slow, precise process of candle-making. If I was tempted to take a short cut, Con stepped in and insisted that we observe the correct process, which paid off in the end as we produced perfectly formed honey-coloured candles. When lit, they had a balanced flame and filled the room with their calming scent. Any undertaking that Con took on had the hallmarks of perfection.

In the early 1970s, due to ill-health, Uncle Jacky semi-retired from the family business, and this increased the workload on Gabriel. This meant that I needed to spend more time in the shop; meanwhile, our three sons had increased to four, so things were busier on the home front as well. Work had to be pruned back and the guesthouse was the obvious place, so we closed it, but Con remained with us. He was now so much part of the family that we could not imagine our lives without him. He was a quiet pool of calm in the midst of our busy household. Then, in the late 1970s, our house was filled with delight when a little girl arrived on the scene. Aunty Peg had died the previous March, shortly after Uncle Jacky, and she had always regretted that there was no girl in our family. So, in many ways I felt that this was their gift. She was christened Lena Shelia Máiréad to cover her two grandmothers and Aunty Peg.

From the first day that she came home from the nursing home, Lena and Con became inseparable. He talked to her when her only response was a gurgle, and as soon as she could form words, she christened him

Condy, and so he remained during her growing years. Because Gabriel and I were often busy in the shop, Con became her foster parent. He read her stories and took her for drives in his car. They went to the beach together when she was barely able to waddle into the water, and he passed on to her his love of the sea. One of the first films they watched together on TV was *Titanic*, and halfway through the film, when the ship was destined to sink, Con heard loud sobs coming from the couch beside him. From this developed a huge mutual interest in the *Titanic*, and the subsequent buying of many books on the subject.

Books became a bone of contention between the two of them as they went to Cork bookshops many Saturdays and she later complained that he was enough to turn her off books because she spent so many hours of her childhood sitting on the doorsteps of bookshops while he selected books. Con had an insatiable thirst for books and it was his one great extravagance. He could not resist a well-bound, well-presented volume on any subject that was of interest to him, and as he had varied interests, it led to the purchase of many books. He always examined hardback editions to see if they were stitched, as he disliked glued books. It was a joy to visit a bookshop with him because he was never in a hurry, something to which Lena as a child strongly objected, but often she was coaxed into toleration with the promise of a later treat.

Even though he taught Maths and Science at St Brogan's, Con was also gifted with his hands, and one of his first creations was a doll's house for Lena, which

Santa brought one Christmas. Early on the morning of that Christmas Eve, Con and I visited an old cottage that he was restoring outside the village. There, in the grey dawn, he put the finishing touches to the doll's house which later that night was to appear in perfect condition under the Christmas tree. Because it was large enough to house many dolls and other bits and pieces it provided years of playing and became part of her bedroom furniture. It was many years before she discovered that Con was the Santa who had made her doll's house.

When our kitchen table, which we had inherited from my sister, began to disintegrate, Con decided to design and make a new one. The plan was for a table large enough to seat our extended household. Our numbers varied but were never small because, as well as ourselves and Con and visiting family and friends, the staff from the adjoining shop often came in to eat. I declared that the table had to be solid, firm and look good. "A tall order," he told me.

When the table was made, it filled all the required specifications. It had the happy knack of not being too large for two or three but still able to sit twelve if necessary. Afterwards Con made a work bench for the back porch, which turned this corner into a workshop for the making of beehives and the repair of miscellaneous objects for the house and the children.

As the boys grew up, Con became a friend and adviser, and when Gearóid and Diarmuid came to secondary-school age, they travelled to St Brogan's with him; when Seán later studied history, the two of them enjoyed long and complicated discussions about ancient civilisations. Con was always amused by the fact that in family discussion where heated exchanges often took place, our eldest, Micheal, never used two words where one would do.

At the age of eight, Lena took up horse riding, and Con often drove her to the local stables. On going back to collect her, he would wait patiently while her friend Sage was bedded down for the night. When she started into competitive riding and tack had to be polished, he never objected if saddles and bridles were strewn around his feet, emitting aroma of horse, as he watched the nightly news on TV. Her brothers were not as tolerant, but if an argument ensued, Con backed Lena up, and if that situation was reversed, she was in his corner.

Many problems that arose during her teenage years were discussed with Con, and often it was months later that Gabriel and I heard of something that had worried her. All her school subject choices and problems were sorted between the two of them as they travelled together every day before he dropped her off at her convent school in Bandon. They decided on her choice of course in UCC and the points necessary to get it, and on the day when her Leaving Cert results came out, she and I collected them in the morning but they remained unopened on the kitchen table until Con came from school that evening. Gabriel and I could understand her need for Con to be there, as they had shared the preparation and now she wanted him there for the results, be they good or bad. Fortunately they were good and both were equally thrilled.

Over the years, Con had become the tried and trusted friend of the whole family, and Gabriel and he often laughed when they recalled the first day he had come and my announcement that he could stay for only a week.

Since then, he had become one of us. Because he was so closely woven into the family fabric, he was immersed in all our ups and downs and was often the one to pour oil on troubled waters. He was completely non-judgmental. At the other end of the scale, we had a family member who thought that the main aim of the rest of us was to make his life a misery. The result was that when that relation visited, we all bent over backwards not to say the wrong thing. After one such visit, as we all breathed a collective sigh of relief, Con said quietly: "Now we can all go back to being ourselves."

When Gabriel and I first visited Kenny's bookshop in Galway, we knew straight away that this would be Con's idea of heaven. I had to travel the country every time I had a new book out, to do signings at bookshops, so any time I had a book signing in Galway, Con and I set off early in the morning so that he could enjoy a long day in Kenny's. He loved that shop and always smiled ruefully before setting out for Galway, declaring that it was going to be an expensive visit. He knew that he could never resist the wonderful old books on offer. When we visited Kenny's during the summer of 2000, he brought along his old copy of the Rev.

Diggs bible on beekeeping, *The Practical Bee Guide*, to have it bound in hardback.

Just before that Christmas, Con got what we thought was a bad flu, but Ellen, my sister, who is a nurse and was home from Canada, insisted that he go to the doctor, who sent him to hospital for a check-up. The result of the tests was shattering: terminal cancer, with a very short projected lifespan. Medically there was nothing to be done, and Con came home two days before Christmas for what we believed might be at least a few months, though we were hoping for longer and praying for a miracle.

His two brothers, Fr Denis and Fr Pat, came to spend Christmas with us, knowing that it would be their last with Con. Like Con, they are gentle and unassuming. It was a Christmas full of pain, spirituality and an awareness that we were walking on the edge of a precipice.

We knew that we would be able to take good care of Con at home because we had medical expertise in the house, Fr Denis being a doctor and Ellen a nurse. But, in the event, long-term care was not required as Con died on 3 January 2001. His death, like his life, was full of peace and tranquillity.

Con's illness and death had all happened so quickly that many of his fellow teachers and students in St Brogan's, where he had taught up to the Christmas holidays, were taken completely unawares. They poured into our front room with grief-stricken faces, and stood beside his coffin where he was laid out in his best grey suit. His coffin, surrounded by lit candles in Aunty

Peg's brass candlesticks, stood in the corner where for many years he had sat correcting exam papers, reading his books or doing the *Irish Times* crossword. It was heart-breaking to see his young students gaze unbelieving into the coffin at the teacher they had loved. For all of us it was a cruel blow, but my heart bled especially for Lena, to whom he had been a loving friend and mentor.

Friends took over the kitchen and fed all comers. The neighbours who had known and loved Con, and the members of the local bridge club where he had been a member for many years, all came to say goodbye. Even though he had been a blow-in like myself, he had become very much part of parish life.

The following evening, through a cold, bleak January landscape, we followed his hearse back along the road through Macroom and Carriganima to his home in Boherbue where he was laid to rest beside his parents. Our great grandmothers had been sisters and it was that family connection that had brought him to Innishannon the first day. Over the years, he had enriched our home with many blessings.

Afterwards

His room
A book
The story
Of his life.
Each crevice
Filled to capacity,
A beehive
Of remembrances.
A collector
Of coins
Family history
Rare books
And stamps.
His room.
As his life
A book of interest.
I turned back
The pages of his life
Back to his childhood
This man's treasure
His love of little things
I walked on sacred ground
Back through his years.

CHAPTER
FOUR

Decades of Damp

His intense concentration on his surroundings caught my attention. He was not in my direct line of vision but slightly to my right as he sat in front of me at mass. His eyes roamed around the church. He began with the sanctuary area, taking in the blotched walls. I watched him out of the corner of my eye. Up and down his glance swept like a giant brush along the walls, and then his eyes locked on to a patch in the middle of the stained-glass window, above the altar. I recognised his problem. It was very difficult to be sure if it was the stained glass or the real sky that boasted that particular shade of blue. I felt tempted to lean forward and assure him, "It is a hole." But I knew when he nodded his head thoughtfully that he had figured it out for himself.

Then he moved down along the aisle walls where navy-blue and grey mildew had battled through layers of ancient green plaster. The plaster had surrendered many years previously. He noted the cracks in the latticed windows and the frayed sash ropes swaying aimlessly in mid-air, and then he tilted back his head and took in the arching ceiling with its fractured cornice mouldings and grey cobwebs hanging lankly from high-flying bulbs. When these bulbs needed to be replaced, it was necessary to erect scaffolding, or a brave parishioner — usually Gabriel — tied two tall ladders together and risked life and limb to replace them.

After mass I waited for our visitor to leave the church. I followed him down the aisle as he tilted back his head to take in the sloping overhead gallery where exposed rotted rafters crawled like black snakes along the gaping ceiling. In the back porch he frowned at a modern PVC window in an old gothic arch. As he came out the door I knew that any attention he might have given to the ceremony had been overwhelmed by the condition of our parish church.

Suddenly he turned and caught my eye: "Are you the woman who writes the books?" he demanded, and when I nodded, he shook his head and informed me grimly: "Ye have a lovely little village but ye'r church is a bloody disgrace!"

I could not contradict him. It was an embarrassment at funerals and weddings to watch outsiders look around our church in disbelief. After all, ours was not a poor parish. Brides before they walked up the aisle fought bravely to improve the look of the place, but it is difficult to put a good face on a tired old lady whose bone structure has collapsed. One posh prospective bridegroom had inquired in a plummy English accent: "Could one not give this place a lick of paint before one commences proceedings?" Unfortunately we were long gone past the remedy of a quick lick of paint.

There is nothing more likely to cause trouble in any parish than the restoration of the parish church. Because it is everybody's church it is everybody's business, and even if you never darken the door of the place it is still your church. We all know what is best for this place where we were baptised, got our first holy communion and were possibly married — though that could be a double-edged sword. Above all, the chances are that when our race is run it is in here we will be brought for a final farewell. So this is our place and doing it up is akin to doing up the family home. We all need to air our opinion, to have it heard and acknowledged. The man in charge of this job is usually the parish priest, and for his future peace of mind he had better get it right.

It so happened that in our parish, just as we were finally about to get moving on church restoration, we got a new parish priest. We knew nothing about him so he had that advantage. He had rubbed nobody up the wrong way by forgetting to call out an anniversary or by not agreeing a time for a baptism. He was starting with a clean sheet. How it would be when the restoration was over would depend on his tact, his delegation skills and his ability to suffer us all gladly. It would also depend on how he handled our funerals. The bereaved are vulnerable and a priest who is sensitive and caring around death will be forgiven many other flaws. But as yet our new PP was an unopened package, so I rang my friend Noeleen who had worked with him in his previous parish and asked, "What kind is the new fella?" I could sense her smiling over the phone as she told me: "He won't put a foot wrong." Well, I thought to myself, that will be some achievement.

A small building committee had been set up by the previous priest. We were just five in number because he believed that small is beautiful. I was on this committee with no commendation other than a deep love of and attachment to this old church that was built in 1829. The plot had been given by the local landlord, which was a very generous gesture for the time and had caused certain ripples of disquiet amongst the landed gentry who would not be attending that church. The wily parish priest of that time, fearing a change of mind that could lead to a claw-back of his plot, buried the first four coffins at its four corners. At that time nobody moved the dead.

I was not baptised here and had not received my first holy communion here, so I was a blow-in. But the chances were that I would be carried in here for my grand finale because many years previously Aunty Peg, in her wisdom, had bought a family grave by the main pathway, commenting: "If I'm there beside the path someone will see me and say a prayer." One day I will join Aunty Peg and Uncle Jacky in their sunny patch. So I had a vested interest.

We had meetings with architects, lighting designers, heating experts, sound experts, stone experts and endless other experts and people who were no experts at all. But it was good for me to have a demanding project on hand because Con's death had rocked the ground beneath our feet. The meetings went on for months and months and we had meetings about meetings. And in the meanwhile parishioners asked, "What are ye doing? When is it ever going to start? How much will it cost?"

The day the quantity surveyor finally came up with the cost was the day I nearly fell off the chair with shock. For some reason I had got it into my head that we could be talking about £500,000 and I had thought that even that was a very sizeable sum. So when the quantity surveyor calmly threw out a figure of a million I realised that we had one big problem.

Now, this was a few years before millions began to be thrown around like snuff at a wake, and it remained a million even after we had pared the cost back to the bone. In the original plan there had been extra details that we had cut out. I repeated a million to myself a few times just to get used to the sound of it: a million . . . a million . . . a million. The parish would have to raise a million. There is nothing that concentrates the mind of a parish like a million. Once the figure had sunk into my mind, I concluded that it was a case of getting the money and getting the job done, but it soon became apparent that there would be more to it than that.

At one of our endless meetings, Fr Tom Hayes from the bishop's office came to discuss matters. He was pleasant, enthusiastic and full of good ideas. He pointed out that the money would restore the building but that the actual fundraising itself could revitalise our parish. That possibility had never dawned on me, but I could see his logic. After all, what good was a beautiful building with no sense of community? To me his was a whole new concept that turned on a light in my head.

55

But a week later, when on a wet dismal night a group of us came together around the altar in St Mary's to form a finance committee, that light flickered. We seemed to be a disorganised, ill-assorted collection, all wondering where to begin, and the gloomy church added to our sense of depression. The prospect of trying to transform this damp old building into a place of warmth and comfort was a daunting one. Like many old churches around the country, it was cold, bleak and miserable, and certainly not serving the purpose for which it was intended.

I was at this finance meeting to represent the building committee. Members of the building committee had decided at a previous meeting that we should not be on the two committees. If you were on too many committees in any parish, the people who did nothing might decide very quickly that you were trying to run the parish. So one committee was enough. When a determined man decided that I should be PRO, I protested and informed him that as I was already on the building committee, I could not be on the finance committee. "Says who?" he demanded. My protestations were swept aside and I was told that if I was helping to spend the money, then I should be helping to make it as well. There was no arguing with that logic. Gabriel, who had served here as an altar boy, was also on both committees, and the restoration of this church was one of his life-long ambitions.

So, with stops and starts, the finance committee was gradually formed and the most prevalent feeling that night around the altar was a huge sense of responsibility. At last we had our committee, and though we were all unsure of what lay ahead, we were determined to give it our best. If motivation was needed, it was all around in the dismal peeling walls and leaking steeple of St Mary's. Would our little army be up to the challenge? We would need to pull in all the parish troops.

The structure of a parish is good scaffolding for holding together a community. The station areas within our parish comprise a small number of townlands, and within these station areas the houses rotate the hosting of mass for the neighbouring houses. Apart from the religious aspect, it is the ideal conduit for new people in an area to get to know their neighbours and also to keep the old neighbours in touch with each other.

With the decline of farming in rural Ireland, occasions for meeting up have disappeared. The creamery had always been a great meeting place where farmers waited in line and discussed world events, national events and local happenings. But the creamery disappeared and with it a social corner of rural Ireland. Then the forge where farmers met on wet days to get their horses shod disappeared and then, like falling dominoes, went the local barracks, school and post office. Now the local shop is under threat and the shopkeepers' slogan could be "use us or lose us", and the loss can have a cumulative effect on the community. Some say that big is best, but we are discovering that big is also impersonal and lonely.

So, the stations are one of the networks that thread our parish life together. After the station mass, people sit, chat and eat, and how elaborate the eats are depends solely on each householder, but the usual is tea and cake. Within each station area are people who are interested in maintaining a community structure, and these are the men and women who the people in each station area like to represent them. So, the townland representatives were called to the first collectors' meeting. But would the troops come?

That night, as I walked up the hill to the meeting room in the school, I thought that this was the test. Would we have a good turnout, or would we get off to a dispiriting start? As I rounded the corner, the answer was laid out before me. The road up to the church, the school car park and the church car park were packed with cars. I felt my heart rise. It was good to know that there was life blood pulsing through the veins of our parish.

It was a vibrant meeting with the usual ups and downs, and the people who thought that it was asking too much of the parish, and the people who thought that it was only a question of forging ahead. But meetings are strange events and one negative thinker can turn a whole meeting upside down. When this appeared to be happening, my heart sank. But then a young man whom I did not know stood up at the back of the hall and said with quiet determination: "Let's get one thing clear here right now: we must stop apologising for looking for money for our church. We need the church for baptisms, for communions, weddings and when we die. We're only looking for five pounds a week or whatever people want to give. It's

58

their church and it's up to the people." There was no arguing with such common sense. With his positive statement, he turned the meeting right around. We concluded on a positive note. The parish collection was about to take off. We were on our way!

CHAPTER
FIVE

More than the Money

The backbone of any church fundraising has to be the parish collection. Each parish does it differently but we did ours by townlands. It would be collected in envelopes distributed by the collectors and could be contributed to weekly, monthly or yearly. While guidelines were given regarding the amount, it was totally at the discretion of the contributor. The collectors who lived in each townland would distribute the special envelopes to their neighbours and then collect them about a week later. Some people could choose a direct debit system. Each year there would be a collectors' meeting to bring people together for discussion, to iron out any problems and hand out the collectors' envelopes already sorted into the different townlands. These envelopes could have been delivered by post but this would have taken away the connectedness that is an essential part of a living parish. In today's rural Ireland neighbours can live in total isolation from each other and any exercise that keeps us in touch with each other helps to ease that sense of loneliness that is now part of the rural landscape.

The finance committee felt that special fundraising events could spread the financial burden more evenly across the parish, as well as bringing people together and also enticing in outside support. It would also give people something in return for their money. At the first collectors' meeting it was decided to have a Festival of Flowers. We sent out letters to local flower shops, flower clubs and flower enthusiasts, inviting them to be part of the festival. The response was immediate and generous. Everyone interested in gardening and flowers came together in a common bond. A flower festival is celebratory and uplifting and brings out the best in a parish.

The venue was to be the lovely little chapel of St Patrick's Upton, which lies in the centre of the parish. St Patrick's was the monastery of the Rosminian order which had originally been an orphanage and is now a home for mentally handicapped adults. The chapel here had escaped the rigours of post-Vatican II enthusiasm and had retained its original features so was the ideal place for a flower festival, the theme of which was to be the Joy of Creation, and what better month in which to celebrate this than the month of May.

At the first of many meetings, two groups were formed: the catering group and the flower-arranging group. As with any such undertaking, much discussion, difference of opinion and decision-making followed but one piece of advice carried the day. Kay, who owns a flower shop and had been part of many such fundraising events, sat quietly and listened to the discussions but when we appeared to be going around in all directions and getting nowhere she said quietly: "There are only two things we need to remember: people cannot come if they do not know about it, and when they do come we must make sure that it is worth their while." She put it in a nutshell.

So the wheels began to turn and Margaret took on the organisation of the catering, and Hazel and John the flower show. There was a lot of work in the preparation of the church but a small crew of men brought in sheets of timber and placed them across the seats to provide bases for the floral displays, and they were also at the beck and call of the flower arrangers to haul in large pieces of driftwood and lift sizeable statues. Preparing for a flower festival, we soon learned, is not for the faint-hearted or the argumentative!

The evening before the opening, it was difficult to imagine that out of the surrounding chaos would emerge a flower festival ready to be opened the following night. Mountains of greenery blocked the aisle, ivy was draped over seats, water nymphs that were supposed to peer into water fountains fell headlong into them, and irate ladies searched under seats for pruners intent on getting lost. The birthing of a flower festival is a site strewn with unexploded missiles. But on the Friday it all gradually came together and, ten minutes before the official opening, order was restored. Flower-arrangers are a great crew. While their creative juices are flowing, they can work in total disorder, and then slowly out of the chaos comes a beautiful creation and within a short time the surrounding debris disappears. But while the creative juices are coming to the surface, it is best not to intervene.

The staircase up to the choir gallery at the back of the church was intertwined with floral garlands and the gallery itself was transformed into a woodland of streams, trees, wild flowers and little animals. It was a scene from *The Wind in the Willows*. Up along the church each stand had a different theme and its story was told in flowers with all kinds of imaginative interpretations. The journey around the church needed to be made slowly to absorb the depth and subtle undertones of each display: a scented voyage of delightful discovery. The sanctuary area, being the focal point at the top of the church, brought the voyage to a brilliant finale of intermingling tones waltzing in harmony with the wonderful colour of the overhead stained-glass window. In contrast to the richly colourful story told around the church, the little prayer room off the sanctuary was a tranquil pool of white flowers and lighted candles. People, on entering, immediately fell silent and smiled in appreciation as they were embraced by candlelight, scent and peace. When one woman who could talk for the parish came in and fell silent, I knew that a miracle had happened.

The official opening on the Friday night was performed by Charlie Wilkins, the gardening correspondent of the *Irish Examiner*. Charlie was the ideal choice because tempered with his love of gardening is an irreverent sense of fun, so the opening was both enlightening and entertaining. He was probably the reason why many present were gardeners because his weekly column is addictive and brainwashes you into thinking that time spent other than in the garden is wasted. He is encouraging and dispenses no-nonsense information that turns gardening into a delightful pastime. After the opening, people wandered around the church, viewing and discussing the arrangements. Later, they filed out the back door and drifted across the yard to where the catering team served teas and home-made eats.

Saturday was bright and sunny and all day a steady stream of people walked around the church and afterwards went for tea in a sunlit conservatory where they basked in sunshine. Some people moved at a very slow pace from arrangement to arrangement and studied every last detail with great concentration, and for them a festival of flowers was an occasion to be savoured. For others, however, it was all about the chat, the tea and homemade goodies. But for all it was a leisurely day out, a time to celebrate doing nothing and to meet the neighbours.

During Saturday there was the space and time to enjoy the entire experience but on Sunday crowds poured in and we had to appoint marshals to direct people in an ongoing flow up the church, along a side corridor, out the back door and across the yard for teas. I happened to be at the foot of the altar directing people into the prayer room when I noticed a man coming up the aisle. I have no idea why he stood out but probably it was the intensity of his expression. When he reached me, he said, "This is a strange day for me because my father was reared in the orphanage here and we grew up hearing about Upton, but I have never been here until today." Because I was surrounded by milling people and my job was to prevent a bottleneck, not create one, there was no chance to talk with him. He hurriedly wrote his telephone number on the only thing that I had in my pocket, which was a matchbox. Later that day, somebody came along in a panic looking for matches to light candles, and I parted with my box. Despite trying to trace it later, I never again saw the box of matches. It was something that I deeply regretted because I felt that that man had a story that needed to be told. I wished that I could have gone into the prayer room and, sitting in that quiet place, listened to his story. It is probably one of the greatest problems of today's Ireland that we have no time to listen to each other, and as a result counselling services have had to replace supportive neighbours all around the country.

The flower festival was a great financial success and set the fundraising off to a good start. There is nothing more uplifting than flowers, and a festival of flowers imbues a whole parish with a sense of well-being. As I wrote in a poem called "Fresh Flowers":

Give me a bunch
Of dew-fresh flowers,
What if they will not last:
I cannot live in the future
The present is all I ask.

After celebrating the Joys of Creation in the flower festival we decided to celebrate the past by taking the village back in time. We had a Folk Day in the Bleach and brought the whole village on a walk into the past. Our GAA pitch is known as the Bleach because in 1760 the then landlord, Adderley, brought in a colony of French Huguenots to start a linen and silk industry and the riverside field was used to bleach the linen.

In the windows along the village, householders put out old photographs, oil lamps, butter spades and wash boards. Items on display ranged from decorative chamber pots to ancient hat-pins and studs; studs, in the 1930s, were used to keep your shirt on. Viewers walked along, looking at the old photographs, and had great fun remembering the uses for all the old tools. As they came up the village towards the Bleach, they heard the nostalgic hum of the threshing machine, and when they arrived at the Bleach gate, they were met by ladies in Victorian dress.

Inside the gate, the thresher pumped out golden straw while men in studded shirts, caps and braces fed it with corn. Along the field, women in gingham dresses made brown bread and baked it in the old-style bastable, while others made butter. The children were delighted with the animal corner of hens, chickens and donkeys. On the back of a lorry, a group of traditional musicians played Irish sets and old time waltzes for people who danced on a wooden platform which was the dance floor of an earlier time. Along by the river, rows of vintage cars and tractors brought great enjoyment to the farmers who remembered the way it used to be. A large army tent was the shop counter for the entire Folk Day and from it cakes, jams and all kinds of home produce were dished out by ladies in floppy hats and starched white aprons.

Across the road from the Bleach is the Church of Ireland church, and on the front lawn ladies dressed in elegant finery served tea to the reverend ministers of both churches. The table was draped with a lace cloth, and tea was poured from a silver teapot into fine bone china and served with cucumber sandwiches and iced sponge cakes. It was a little cameo from an earlier time when gracious living was the order of the day. All these leisurely scenes were acted out as fast-moving traffic thundered relentlessly through our small village, but for just one day the whole parish enjoyed a leisurely trip down memory lane.

CHAPTER
SIX

My Two Wise Men

"What are you looking for?" the builder demanded.

"Two wise men," I told him hesitantly.

"Hard job that now," he informed me. "They could be scarce."

"Well, they were here," I said, stubbornly poking around in the rubble.

"When?" he demanded.

"About two years ago, I think, was the last time I saw them," I told him vaguely. "They were part of the old crib."

"Missus, what planet are you off?" he demanded in amazement, rolling his eyes to heaven. "Don't you know that everything 'walks' nowadays?" Then he had second thoughts: "Although wise men could be left. There would be few people needing them. No place for wise men in today's world."

We were up in the gallery of St Mary's, our church that was being restored. It had been vacated months previously when we moved down into Christ Church. Our Church of Ireland brethren had very generously offered us the use of their church, and St Mary's was now a building site and anything of value had been cleared off site — with the exception of the missing wise men; but apparently not everybody considered them very valuable.

When you came up the circular iron staircase that curved into the gallery, and stepped on to the wooden floor, the prevailing smell was of mould and rotting wood. Climbing up the tiered gallery it was necessary to watch your step as you edged around an accumulation of odds and ends that had been dumped there over the years. If we were encumbered down in the church with shaky seats, odd vases or any homeless article, they were carried up to the gallery, and it was a case of out of sight, out of mind.

In the early 1960s, the parish had invested in a new set of crib figures. Nurse Murphy, who had been district nurse here for years and had always looked after the crib, had decided we needed a new set of figures and had a quick whip-around to pay for them. The new figures were bright, light and very mobile, whereas the old plaster ones were solid and cumbersome. The old set was relegated to the gallery where, on a deep windowsill at the back, a year-round crib was created. Over the years I had sometimes seen them and had vaguely noted that they were decreasing in number, and in recent years all that remained were the two wise men

In some way, that crib had appealed to the long-lost child in me because it was a replica of the crib in the church in North Cork where I had dropped in my brown pennies on Christmas morning. I remembered hoping that Holy Mary would buy some warm clothes for the baby with my money.

Now I looked around the gallery that was strewn with planks and an assortment of miscellaneous rubbish. I struggled to the windowsill, carefully picking my steps in between old heaters and dehumidifiers, but my journey was in vain, as the deep sill housed only torn hymn books and a broken kneeler. Now, where were my two wise men? Or had they walked? Maybe not, because on last sighting they were in a bad state. Very few would have wanted them in that condition. Maybe they were left there in the first place because they were not as appealing as the others. Everyone would have wanted Mary and even Joseph, and of course the Baby Jesus was probably first out the door, and there is something very nice about a spare donkey, not to mention an extra cow; the shepherds and sheep, too, would have added a yuletide atmosphere to any Christmas scene. But no one must have felt the need to take home a haughty king in a long dress, not to mention a black one with a gold ear-ring. So, perhaps they had just slowly crumbled in the damp.

"What's going to happen to them if they are still here?" I asked.

"Skip," he informed me.

"I'm taking them," I told him.

"Well, I'm sure no one will outbid you," he answered smartly.

"But first we must find them," I told him.

"You mean, *you* must find them," he pronounced as he clattered down the gallery stairs.

I pulled and dragged planks of timber and broken seats, disturbing long-legged black spiders who for years had had undisputed possession. An ancient organ would not be moved so I went down on my hands and knees to peer under it, but all that was to be seen was a mummified mouse. He had probably died of pneumonia or of hunger and he was not a very smart mouse to have been up here in the first place. Then it dawned on me that if a mouse had found his way up here, so too could a rat, and a shudder ran down my spine. From then on, I moved things gingerly, in nervous anticipation, but when I peered between the organ and the wall and saw a gold earring glint in the shadows, I had to take my courage in both hands and reach into the darkness and haul out a heavy black king by the scruff of the neck. He was minus one leg and had a gaping hole in his backbone. The back of his head had crumbled and he was minus all regal garb. But his remains were all mine, and the chances were that his travelling companion could be somewhere as well.

I found the second king in a far worse state than the first because he had no head at all. I searched around for his lost head but it was nowhere to be found. I felt that the head had to be around somewhere so I searched on doggedly and all fear of rats dead or alive evaporated in my determination to find the lost head. As the search continued, my builder friend clattered up the stairs.

"Any luck?" he inquired with a smirk on his face.

"I'm looking for a head," I told him.

"Yerra, half the country is functioning without one of them," he told me. "What would an ould king want one for?"

"Still, he'd look better with it," I informed him.

"Maybe," he agreed; "though I see some faces around here and people would be better off without them."

I decided at this point that he was not very sympathetic to my situation, but I was too quick in my judgment because just then he shifted a kneeler and there was the head, or rather half a head, as all the poor king had was a face with nothing behind it. My friend was off again.

"Just the job," he declared. "Most people are operating with half a head anyway."

"I'm going to restore him," I informed him smugly.

"There's one born every day," he declared, shaking his head at the stupidity of his fellow humans.

"Will you help me carry them down the stairs?" I requested.

"Missus, you don't need two wise men; you need two strong men."

But despite his protestations he manoeuvred the two battered wise men down the winding narrow stairs.

They were heavy so I brought up the wheelbarrow to carry them and their spare parts down the hill to their new home. I steered the wheelbarrow in the back door, wrapped my arms around each king in turn and eased him on to the hall table. It was probably as near as I would ever come to hugging a royal. However, these were two weighty royals and each move tested the strength of my muscles.

When they were anchored on the table, I stood back and surveyed them. They were a sorry sight but one day they must have been quite beautiful. They had been forced to abdicate in the mid-1960s and had been in the crib for about forty years before that, so my two kings were almost one hundred years old. And they looked every year of it! I brought out the Hoover and sucked all the dust off their outsides and then went down the throat of the headless one and cleaned out his insides. Then I rang a local potter about the possibility of moulding a head for my wise man, but I knew after a short conversation that he did not consider it a viable project and wanted to get rid of me. It would have to be a "little red hen" job.

It was the week before Christmas and, as I drew in holly from the garden to decorate the house, the two wise men kept an eye on my comings and goings, and as the days passed by, the memory of their counterparts in the church of my childhood began to come alive in my mind. Each caller to the house was taken to visit the two wise men. Their original roles were reversed and, instead of being the royal visitors to the crib, they were now the visited. On Christmas Eve, they guarded the stuffed turkey as she waited for her big day, and later when I lit the usual Christmas candle on the back window, they waited in the shadows. Their day was about to dawn.

After the Christmas dinner, I dragged my two wise men up to the attic where I while away many hours pretending that I am an artist. I had big plans for them but I was also open to inspiration from them. My sister Ellen, who also likes to paint, decided to adopt one of them. I parted with the small black fellow sporting the traces of a gold ear-ring. The evidence that he was originally black was pitted around his elbow and knee while the rest of him was a sludge grey.

Our first problem was to give my wise man a new head and a new foot, but the head was the big problem. Amazingly enough, with a wooden spoon down his neck and an Irish linen tea towel for a brain, he was moulded into shape with a wonderful gun-full of gooey clay. When the back of his head had been shaped and covered with long flowing hair his face was put into position. When the clay dried, his face was secure and he had a sound head on his shoulders. With similar methods we created a leg and he finished up with a well-turned ankle and five elegant toes. With all his body parts in position the next step was to drape him in royal finery.

Once we started mixing paints, memories of the wise men of my childhood crib began to awaken and I felt as I painted that the colour scheme was almost decided by memory, and the royal man himself influenced my decision as well. When he was finally dressed, he was resplendent in a glowing robe and crimson cloak, with a golden crown on his black flowing tresses, and holding a jewelled casket of frankincense between his elegant royal fingers. His dark companion turned out as handsome but, while my royal was upright and bearing gifts, his friend was down on one knee and in obvious awe at some unseen wonder. He was dark and intriguing and full of eastern mystery, and his ear-ring glistened with newly polished gold. Their restoration had been a journey back to the old crib, a journey full of the challenge that had made Christmas easier. This was our first Christmas without Con and I was learning that creativity is part of the healing process.

Having restored the two wise men, I had to decide what to do with them. Nobody, it seemed, felt in need of two ancient kings. But our house is old and roomy and over the years an assortment of odds and ends has accumulated, so two wise men would not be out of place. At each side of our front door are two half pillars and these were the perfect perches for them. So now a pair of retired kings guards our front door.

CHAPTER
SEVEN

Will You Buy a Ticket?

Selling tickets is not for the faint-hearted. The local garage gave the parish the gift of a car, and the finance committee felt that we needed to go outside the parish to sell sufficient tickets. The decision about the price of the raffle ticket led to long and protracted discussions, with some people thinking that €5 was enough and others going for €20. After much argument and counter-argument a conclusion was finally reached and it came down on the side of €20. So then began the programme of events known as "Will you buy a ticket?"

It turned out to be an experience from which I learnt many things. The first was that the media do not always represent the thinking of the ordinary people and that the chattering minority obliterates the silent majority. The country was awash with the scandal of clerical abuse and we were very apprehensive about the reception we would receive when we went out selling tickets in aid of church restoration. But we discovered that the people did not hold the majority of priests guilty for the sins of the few. They saw the church as belonging to them and many times greeted us with the comment:

"Oh, we must support the church!" That was the first surprise, and there were many more to follow.

Our first venue was the Innishannon Steam Rally, which is held every June bank holiday weekend and draws crowds from all around the country. There is a huge interest in vintage steam engines, and once a year all the faithful pour into our parish. We enthusiastically set up a table beside our shining new car at the best vantage point in the rally field; after all, it was our parish and we, of course, demanded the prime location.

Our car was surrounded by vibrant posters proclaiming the wonders of winning a brand-new model for only €20, and we waited full of happy anticipation for the eager buyers to line up. But we waited and waited and waited. Only a tiny minority of the flowing tide of people ventured in our direction. We were discovering that if you go fishing, the fish do not come looking for your bait! You have to cast your net out into the deep. So up we got up off our backsides and sallied out into the flowing throngs, offering our wares and engaging people in conversation.

The first step in selling tickets is that you have to *believe* that the populace is lucky to get this opportunity to buy your ticket and, having convinced yourself of that, you must then convince the punter. You quickly learn to read faces, but you discover as you go along that it is very easy to get it wrong and that a large, jovial talkative man does not necessarily guarantee that you will have a sale at the end of the conversation. It could be that he just likes the sound of his own voice and, having let many other potential customers pass you by, you discover that though his mouth was open, his wallet was tightly zipped. Sometimes a distracted woman dragging a shoal of children behind her might look an unlikely prospect but she could surprise you and decide to take a sporting chance. We found out that a big heart is always more important than a big wallet. By the third day of the rally, we were no longer green beginners but learning fast the art of selling tickets.

The steam rally provided our launching pad, but it was only the beginning in a long list of venues. John was the man in charge of the entire enterprise and he proved an inspired choice because he was a hard worker who never made hard work out of anything. A day selling tickets with this fast-thinking and witty man was a day was full of fun and hilarity. Having been an active member of Macra na Feirme for many years, which involved chairing a debating team to great success around the country, he was also a life-long ardent member of Fine Gael, so he knew more people than Bertie Ahern, and that is a great plus when you go out selling tickets. To me John seemed to know the whole country, and if he was snookered by an approaching stranger, he would whisper under his breath, "Do you know this fella?" and if I said no, he invariable approached them with the opening salutation "And how are we now?" So whenever I heard that salute I knew that John did not have a clue who the person was, but within minutes he would have solved that problem. The ultimate networker, he invariably knew someone belonging to them or someone from their home place. Needless to mention, he knew the whole Fine Gael fraternity and if one of them did not buy, he looked askance — "And he's one of ours," he'd say in exasperation. But he very seldom drew a blank.

At one venue a pernickety woman challenged us as to the newness of our car, seeing as how we were parading it all around the country. She was determined to pick holes in our project. It was late in the evening and we were too tired to argue with her so we agreed with all her arguments, which drove her mad; eventually in frustration she told us that we were "a right shower of chancers".

As we progressed, we fine-tuned our act and instead of dragging the car around with us, we took posters, which was far easier. We also had an oil painting of the church, which we mounted on an easel, and we discovered that people are very interested in anything mounted on an easel. They regard it as a work in progress, and indeed our church was just that and we had large photographs of the scaffolded steeple to prove it. People were interested in the whole enterprise and enjoyed looking at the painting and photographs and hearing of our fundraising efforts.

The best buyers were the people who had at some point in their own lives sold tickets as a fundraiser. Many of them told us, "Oh, God, we had to do this and it was a tough project." And indeed it was, but with a good positive crew on board we also had a lot of fun.

One of our most enjoyable outings was to Listowel Races. We had arranged with the Listowel Council that we could pitch our camp in the small square where all streets converge, and this placed us in the centre of the crowds on the way to the races. This is the square from which John B. Keane now surveys his town. A racing crowd out for the day are in a jubilant mood and most of them are by nature prepared to take a gamble, so they were our kind of people. We set up our posters, easel and photographs and got ourselves ready for the day; we were blessed with the weather, which was kind. We were in for the long haul as three of us had booked into a local guesthouse and reserve troops were to come down daily from home.

The first day would tell a lot. We had a bonanza! One of the reserves who came down that day was Jane who is a racegoer, and when the punters wanted to know if we had a winner, Jane gave one man Monty's Pass who went on to win. When this man came back that evening, he handed us his betting slip to draw the winnings. It was a magnanimous gesture and we were delighted, but he was gone in the crowd before we could thank him properly. Later that night, he passed on his way to the pub and we asked him about his generosity. "I was born outside this town," he said, "and my family hadn't much but when I got to Dublin I did law at night and now I have my own law firm. This town was good to me and it's good to be good to where you came from. As well as that, it's great to see people going out and making an effort for their own place." That man made my day.

The following morning, Hazel and I were manning the corner when a miserable-looking man approached us and I murmured under my breath to Hazel,

"Nothing doing there anyway." But Hazel, the eternal optimist, approached him and in her lilting accent softly introduced the subject — "Would you like to buy a ticket?" — and much to my amazement his hand slowly made its way into a deep inside pocket where a note detached itself from a wad of its companions; having told Hazel that she was a grand girl, he went on his way, and I learned the lesson that you can never predict a buyer!

As well as races, we attended shows, horse fairs and shopping centres. We covered the Prize Cattle Show in the Green Glens in Millstreet where Noel C. Duggan gave us a prime location and bought our first two tickets. It was a great experience to view those perfectly groomed highly bred cattle that are the models of the bovine world. One normally associates the Green Glens with beautiful horses but there we saw that a well-groomed cow is as elegant as any top-class hunter. Politicians came there to strut their stuff because this is the *crème de la crème* of the dairying industry.

We had a great day at Skibbereen Show and there we had the additional advantage that our parish priest, Fr John, had come to us from Skibbereen. It soon became obvious that he had left good memories behind him in the town as the people were delighted to welcome him back and were generous in their support. It was a lovely sunny day and our site under the shelter of an overhanging hedge had a good view of the entire field.

A cattle show must surely be one of the most deeply satisfying and entertaining ways to spend a day in rural Ireland; its title is actually misleading because it

81

encompasses a flower show, art and crafts display, farm-produce competition and a display of the best farm animals, as well as all the up-to-date farm machinery. People wander around and look at all that is on view and in the process meet the neighbours and old friends whom they may not have seen since the last show. In previous years, every fair-sized town had a cattle show which was referred to simply as "the show", but with the decline in agriculture they have dwindled and with them one of the most welcome social aspects of rural Ireland.

On one of our many outings, we visited a horse fair which necessitated a drive of many miles. On arrival, we experienced quite a culture shock. Horses trotted up and down the street, rearing up in protest at approaching traffic. It was like a scene from the Wild West, and if some of the horses were wild, they were no more so than the people who traversed the town. Tanned, tough-looking men in black vests, with tattoos in all visible areas, led prancing ponies and piebald horses up and down the town, accompanied by women in knee-high white plastic boots, wearing skirts up as far as possible and overflowing tops down as far as possible and brassy blonde hair piled high. They formed a volcanic collection, and it was no surprise to see police on horseback patrolling the streets. You felt that a confrontation could erupt at a moment's notice, and not necessarily with the police.

The fact that we were there selling tickets for church restoration brought amazed looks to many faces, and as the day progressed we could understand their amazement. When we went for a meal, we had to pay at the door before entering the premises, which told a lot about the owner's opinion of the clientele. Three of us joined a bleary-eyed drunk who was already sprawled across the table and, in the process of gathering himself together to make room for us, must have made out through a drunken haze the outline of one man and two women.

"How come," he challenged Fr John in a slurred voice, "you have two women and I can't even get one. Is one the wife and if 'tis, can I have the other one?"

I happened to be the other one, and after I had assured him that I was available and willing to be his he rolled over and dozed off and we had our questionable lunch to the background music of his occasional snore. The takings that day were not great but we had seen a slice of Irish life that had come as a big surprise to me.

All our outings were different and some days people were generous and the selling was easy and other days it was tough going and we came home exhausted. But we met a varied selection of people. One pot-bellied balding man well past his sell-by date wanted our car to do more than just transport him around. He wanted to know if it was a "babe magnet". I did not have the heart to tell him that if that was his line of appeal, he should probably be looking at a Jaguar. One woman took it upon herself to tell us that we had no shame in us to be dragging a car around the country selling tickets. But I was glad to have done it and one thing that I discovered while selling tickets was that a sense of humour was a vital necessity. During the entire proceedings Gabriel was our financial controller who kept track of tickets and returns and before each outing provided change and balanced the books when we returned.

The raffle brought in the princely sum of €98,000, so with a total like that we felt it had been worth our while to have dragged ourselves around the country asking all conditions of men and women "Will you buy a ticket?"

CHAPTER
EIGHT

Through the Eyes
of a Child

It was the week before Christmas and like most of the country I was up to my oxters in baking, writing cards and buying presents. On that particular day, I was whipping trays of mince pies in and out of the oven. A small dark head came around the kitchen door and Dan asked: "Alice, will you take me to do my Christmas shopping tomorrow?"

"I will of, course," I told him with delight. It was a long time since I had taken a six-year-old Christmas shopping.

Dan was the youngest of three boys, and his brothers were teenagers. They lived on a farm outside the village, and this would be his very first solo shopping trip. Taking me along was almost as good as going on his own because I knew that my role was to be that of a silent, agreeable observer.

"I'll come in after school tomorrow evening," he said.

"That will be grand," I told him.

"And I'll have my own money," he informed me firmly before closing the door. I was being told that no interference, financial or otherwise, was expected or acceptable. At six, he might not have the right words to let me know what he wanted but he had other ways of getting his message across.

Next evening, he shot in the side door on his way home from school, flung his school bag into a corner and demanded, "Are you ready?"

"What about eating something, Dan?" I ventured.

"Afterwards," I was told.

We set out for nearby Bandon. Dan sat upright in his seat with a look of intense concentration on his face as he worked out the plan of his shopping campaign.

"I must get presents for Mam, Dad, Bill, Henry and maybe Róisín." Róisín was a baby cousin who spent a lot of time in his house and whom he loved dearly.

I thought that I had better ask the burning question although, having consulted his mother, I already knew the answer. But it was best for our negotiations that Dan have all his cards on my table.

"How much money have you got to spend, Dan?" I inquired.

"Twenty euro," he told me, patting his pocket. "And it's all my own and I'm only spending my own money."

Sound man, I thought! Spending only the money in your pocket was not the national average at Christmas. But five presents out of €20 was going to put us to the pin of our collar. *Tread cautiously now, Alice*, I told myself. *This little lad's feelings and pride cannot be dented on this shopping trip*. But his next comment set alarm bells ringing.

"Alice, I think that Mam would like a dishwasher."

"Do you think so, Dan?" I gasped in consternation.

"Well, maybe," he added, and I breathed a sigh of relief that he was not totally hell-bent on a dishwasher.

As we were walking up the main street of Bandon, I ventured: "Where do you want to do your shopping?"

"The new shopping centre," he told me. "They have a big electrical shop there that sells dishwashers."

"Is that right?" I said weakly as my blood pressure rose. I was not off the hook.

"It's going to be a big surprise for Mam," he told me.

My mind went into overdrive trying to figure out how I was going to get out of this predicament. But no solution came readily to mind. Taking a six-year-old shopping had its hidden hazards. Dan forged ahead of me, his stride full of purposeful intent. There seemed to be no way to divert the impending disappointment. He was so overflowing with enthusiasm for his proposed purchase that it seemed cruel to drown his delight in a flood of reality. He was a firm believer in Santa, and in his heart he was now being Santa to his mother. How could I shatter his wonderful world and tell him that he could not buy a dishwasher for €20? He was charging full steam ahead towards a crash landing. How could I soften it?

Then suddenly the theory that worries are sometimes overcome by events became a reality before my very eyes. Dan slapped on his brakes and I almost fell over him. He came to a standstill in front of the pound-shop window. There in scarlet splendour stood an enormous jovial Santa. His portly presence filled the whole window. I was never in my life so glad to see him. His arms were outstretched in welcome and I almost fell into them. This would test his pulling power! Could he obliterate a dishwasher? Dan was intrigued. His eyes filled with wonder. I watched breathlessly. Santa did the trick! The dishwasher did not stand a chance.

"Do you think that we should try in here first?" he asked breathlessly.

"Well, we could try anyway," I assured him, not wanting to sound too enthusiastic, and praying that the power of the pound shop would swing things. He briskly pushed open the door and silently surveyed the shop. It was a child's paradise packed with Christmas wonder. But Dan was not going to rush into anything. He walked very slowly around the packed shelves, paying intense attention to every item at his eye level and kneeling down to inspect the lower shelves. Then he came to a full stop in front of a little tableau of a farm scene. He studied it intently. There was no comment. Then he resumed his journey and I followed wordlessly, holding my breath.

As I passed the little farm, I glanced down but I kept walking because I did not want to appear over-eager. The price tag was €15. Perfect! But how was this going to work out? We were still only at the contemplation stage. Dan came silently around again and examined a little tool-set. Then he continued. On passing, I glanced down at the tool-set. Five euro. So far so good. He slowed down again as he approached the farm. Then he came to a stand-still. He stood there for a long time and studied the tableau and I studied Dan. There was deep concentration and financial analysis going on in his mind and he frowned at the intensity of the decision-making process. Eventually he began to lay out his budget strategy. No minister for finance ever took his portfolio more seriously.

"Have I enough money for this?" he asked thoughtfully. I was so grateful that we were not looking at a dishwasher.

"You have," I told him.

The deep concentration continued, with his hands buried deep in his pockets. Finally he drew one hand out and placed an index finger on the hens.

"Mam would like them," he pronounced.

"She would," I agreed.

He then moved his finger to the horse.

"Dad would like him," he decided.

"He would," I agreed.

He then moved a finger to the tractor.

"Bill and Henry would like that," he continued.

"They would," I agreed.

He then moved his finger to the dog.

"And Róisín would love him," he finished decidedly.

"She would indeed," I agreed with relief.

Then he looked up at me with a triumphant look on his face and two eyes overflowing with delight.

"That will make them all happy," he declared.

"It sure will," I agreed, though they could never be as happy as I was. But Dan was not finished yet. He retraced his footsteps back to the little tool-set and examined it carefully.

"Have I enough for this?" he queried.

"You have," I assured him.

"Dad and I could work with it," he decided. His father did wood-turning and Dan loved the workshop.

"Now Dad and I will be happy together," he told me.

This minister for finance would leave the opposition speechless!

He carefully picked up his farm set and took it to the checkout and then went back for his tool-set. I maintained my role as a silent observer. He viewed the girl at the checkout.

"Will you wrap my Christmas presents?" he asked her solemnly.

"Of course," she said, smiling, and asked, "Would you like a Santa card?"

There was no need for words as his glowing smile gave the answer. His smile lit up her Christmas spirit and she did a beautiful job on his two presents.

As we left the shop, he whispered to me: "Wasn't she very nice; isn't it nice to be nice?"

Maybe he was not government material after all. We stood and admired the huge red man in the window.

"Isn't Santa magic?" he said with a sigh.

"He is indeed," I agreed wholeheartedly.

After all, he had just turned a dishwasher into a farm.

CHAPTER
NINE

Innishannon Creates It

Within each of us lies a dormant pool of creativity and, when the waters of this well begin to flow, the result can be deep inner fulfilment. Artists, wood-turners, knitters, bakers, embroiderers, and lace-makers are part of this network, as is anyone who creates with their hands and imaginations. They wake up in the morning with minds excited at the prospect of a picture to be painted or a carving to be finished or a tapestry to be completed. Creativity fills them with satisfaction and brings beauty into their lives and the lives of those around them. Such people are to be found in every parish. How many had we in our parish? There was only one way to find out and that was to provide a showcase for their creations. That showcase would be "Innishannon Creates It".

Such a display of quality hand-made goods could not happen overnight. It takes time to create beautiful things, and so in January we laid out our idea to the parish via the church newsletters and local media. Each donated item would be sold at its full value for the church fund. We went to great pains to assure people that their creations would not be undervalued and sold cheaply to bargain-hunters. Hours of loving dedication resulting in beautiful articles deserved to be appreciated and the articles sold for their true value. This was going to be a display of superb quality meriting discerning customers.

There was a hugely positive reaction to the idea from the parishioners; the whole concept caught people's imagination and they got to work. They had the best part of a year for their projects as the following Christmas was targeted as the date when we would actually hold "Innishannon Creates It". During the year we heard tell of patchwork quilts, christening robes, lace cloths, hand-knitted jumpers, paintings and tapestries in the making. We held our breath, hoping that we would have quantity as well as quality, but only time would tell. That was the excitement of doing something for the first time: there was no blueprint, so you could have a runaway success or a complete flop on your hands. Throughout the year we promoted a slow build-up of interest, stimulating the creators and alerting potential purchasers.

During the summer months we collected rose petals from the local gardens and laid them out to dry in the warm sun. When finally dry, they were feathery light with a wonderful array of colour and a heavenly smell. They needed to be well presented and luckily Paddy, who lives outside the village and is always ready to help, had taken up wood-turning and gave us dozens of wooden bowls which we filled with the gorgeous-smelling rose petals. Another parishioner, Claire, had a niece in Chicago whose business was top-quality labelling, and she sent us a roll of specially printed lush gold labels. Bowls of "Innishannon Pot Pourri" would make great Christmas gifts, especially for parish people overseas.

Candles are synonymous with Christmas, so we decided to make pure beeswax candles. Con's beeswax had been carefully stored away and nothing would have pleased him better than to have it used in candles to raise funds for the church that he had loved. So when his brother, Fr Denis, came on holiday, we spent days making candles and our kitchen turned into a candle-making factory. At first, progress was very slow because we lacked Con's know-how and advice, but I remembered some of the details and we purchased a book on candle-making which we consulted as we went along.

We put a heavy saucepan on the Aga and into it went a large dome of yellow wax and the right measure of stearin powder. Ours was seasoned wax with a touch of velvet and rich honey smell. Slowly liquid wax began to ooze from the base of the dome and gently with a wooden spoon we moved the wax around and gradually the dome got smaller and smaller until it had turned into a pot of liquid amber. We kept stirring until the wax was bubbling hot. Then we put a taper into a candle mould and eased it through the hole at the bottom and sealed it with the special sealer, being careful to steady the taper in the centre using a little bit of wood across the top to keep it in place. The next step was to pour some of the boiling wax carefully into the mould, making sure to keep the wick in the centre.

When the mould was almost full, we let the hot wax rest, air bubbles escaped and a little sag formed; we filled this to give an even base to the candle.

At first we did as the book instructed and stood the candle mould in cold water to cool but we discovered that the fridge worked just as well and this made things easier. When the wax had cooled and the candle was set in the mould, we had great difficulty in ejecting it until we discovered the simple trick of putting the mould into the deep freeze for a few minutes and then rolling it between our warm hands until we heard a sharp crack as the wax contracted from the mould. Then the candle came out smooth and creamy. It smelt of pure honey and felt like warm satin. Pure wax candles burn very slowly and give out a rich honey aroma — these were the perfect Christmas candles. Here Paddy weighed in with sturdy wooden candle-sticks around which we tied a red ribbon and Claire's golden labels reading: "Pure beeswax Innishannon candles".

From 1 November onwards, we requested that people begin bringing in their goods. Because our old house is big and rambling with lots of space, and conveniently placed in the centre of the village, we decided to gather everything here in the one place and then we would know exactly what we had on our hands.

It began with a trickle that grew into a stream and as momentum gathered it turned into a flood. Our large front room began to fill up with boxes and bags that gradually overflowed into the corridors and into what we term the *seomra ciúin* (quiet room), which could no longer be so described as people came and went, bringing such beautiful things that I was absolutely gob-smacked. In came wonderful patchwork quilts, one of which was completely hand-stitched; three christening outfits comprising embroidered dresses edged with lace; hand-crocheted robes with matching bootees. Two tapestry pictures of breathtaking beauty, one of which had taken over two years to make — and the generous lady was not even a member of our church but on hearing of "Innishannon Creates It" got it finished by working long hours. Original oils and watercolours came in, and knitwear in all colours and sizes, together with wooden lamps and bowls crafted from seasoned timber of Dromkeen Wood. The standard and quality were tremendous and we knew that we were looking at prospective family heirlooms and collectors' items of the future.

One morning a sturdy box was handed in and when it was opened we knew straight away that this was the work of an expert because the cushions and Christmas stocking were like something to be seen in Harrods. The wonderful lady who had made them had for many years been a seamstress in London and had now retired to the parish.

We built up our advertising campaign using the newsletters of all the churches in the diocese — a wonderful medium of networking for church activities — and we wrote articles for the local papers and mounted advertising boards at both entrances to the village. This was one of the advantages of being on the main road to West Cork as we were in the line of vision of 30,000 vehicles passing daily through our village. In all our advertising we emphasised that these were top-quality articles and would not be cheap, which caused one woman to comment caustically: "Looks like 'twill be no place for bargains!"

The venue was to be Innishannon Hotel, sited just outside the village at the end of a tree-lined drive across the Bandon river from Dromkeen Wood. We had free use of the hotel's large glass-fronted function room overlooking the river and wood. The plan was to run the event on the Saturday and Sunday and to set up the room on the Friday night. But there was a wedding in the hotel on that Friday which would probably go on far into the night. This meant that we would have to set up the room in the small hours of Saturday morning. At 4a.m., as arranged, two large borrowed vans manned by locals pulled up outside our house and willing volunteers loaded up the goods, which had already been segregated into different categories, and when we arrived at the hotel more parishioners were waiting to unload them into the appropriate stalls where others arranged the different displays. We each had a copy of the lay-out and when the long room was finally ready for customers it was an arresting sight. I felt a glow of pride that our small parish had actually produced such a magnificent display.

The fair began at ten o'clock, and by 10.30 the room was packed with people. It was a case of he who hesitates is lost because some people decided to walk around and have a think about the feasibility of a purchase, only to discover on return that a more decisive customer had acquired their object of desire.

By lunchtime, all top-quality items had been sold, and the first items to go had been the two tapestry pictures, which brought in €1,500 between them. Paintings were in great demand and some disappointed customers sought out the artists with requests for similar pictures.

One item caused a bit of excitement. A beautifully knitted snow scene consisting of a fat Santa and two large snowmen was meant to be sold as a complete lot but one customer succeeded in persuading one of our attendants to sell one snowman, and this resulted in a lopsided scene which annoyed another customer who had previously admired it in its entirety and had decided to purchase it. She demanded an explanation for the missing snowman. The attendant was reluctant to face the tribunal and tell the story of the missing snowman, so the annoyed woman sought out the knitter for an explanation, and the knitter came to me for an explanation. But there is no explanation for some things.

A cautious man admired a hand-knitted crib into which one dedicated knitter had put many hours of work. He felt that it would be ideal for his young children but decided that he would have a look around in case there was better value further down the room. But a young teacher from the local primary school knew value when she saw it, declaring:"I can't believe that someone had the patience to knit this whole nativity scene. I'd eat it first! But it's perfect to teach the tiny tots about the crib."

It was deeply satisfying for the creators of all these lovely things to see how much people appreciated their

97

work. It had always surprised me that at sales of work people actually expected to get quality home-made goods cheaper than their mass-produced poorer-quality equivalents. It was an attitude destined to kill any cottage industry.

By Saturday evening, all the large items had been purchased; on Sunday the crowds continued to come, and, by Sunday evening, we were practically sold out. People had travelled long distances and were delighted with the quality of the goods and with the hotel setting where they were able to walk along by the river and then have lunch or afternoon tea in the dining room overlooking the wood and river. By Sunday night, we were all exhausted but delighted that "Innishannon Creates It" had been such a great success. It had brought in €25,000 for the church fund, but more important than the money was the sense of pride that our parish had such a wealth of talent and people who were generous enough to give so much of themselves in time and effort. When pools of creativity are stimulated, an entire parish is enriched.

CHAPTER
TEN

Cleaning Up

In an ancient graveyard at the end of our village stands an old tower dating back to 1225. Early Huguenot settlers, who brought the linen industry to Innishannon, had built a little side chapel on to the church and later some of them were buried there. Over the years the tombs and headstones were covered in bushes and briars and the gate into the graveyard could not be opened as there was a tree growing up through the gate pillar and tangled through the gate. This forgotten graveyard was a prisoner behind a rusty gate crying out for attention.

Early in the summer of 1983 a small group of us came together and began to hack back the smothering overgrowth. We put in long hours of dogged hard work, so much so that one cynical man decided that we must be getting paid for our efforts. "No one in their right mind," he told us, "would do all that for nothing." The cleared debris was piling high beside the gate and one night we set fire to it. At the time, there was no legal restriction on bonfires but there were other forces at large.

An irate lady who lived nearby almost set fire to us with her hot tongue and dire threats of legal proceedings. One of our workgroup was a very genteel clergyman whose ears had never before been assailed by such a verbal onslaught. He there and then decided that the living could render looking after the dead a very dangerous undertaking; he quickly withdrew to the safety of his own residence. Some of us, however, were more accustomed to local hazards, and were prepared to weather the storm. We continued with the nightly effort and uncovered the tombs of the early Huguenots and then began to clear out the side chapel. Having wheeled out many barrows of earth, we finally reached ground level. There, to our amazement, were inscribed flagstones over the tombs that had been buried for decades. It was a strange feeling to read the inscriptions on the long-obscured vaults; we felt a little as if we had discovered hidden treasure. It was the burial place of one family and many of those buried there had been very young.

Some of the tombs around the graveyard had also collapsed and bones were scattered at the entrances. One night when putting old bones back into the tombs we were joined by a group of young people on holiday. The following day, I met a bewildered mother who wanted to know if her teenage son was having her on when he told her that he had spent the previous evening putting bones back into old tombs. It was a bit difficult to put a normal face on this unusual activity. I think that the woman decided that she had come on holiday to a rather strange place.

After the clean-up of the old graveyard we moved on to clearing out the woods. Innishannon is surrounded by beautiful woods with wonderful walks, but these had become blighted by some unseemly sights. As a Tidy Towns project we decided to do something about it, and we appealed for volunteers. The key elements of a good voluntary turn-out are phone calls and knocking on doors, and we reaped our reward in the form of large teams of people from all ages spending several weekends working together to clear the woods of rubbish. We came across all kinds of strange objects, including one bundle consisting of a pair of large pink knickers, a bra and an ancient corset wrapped up in an old towel.

"Do you think," one man asked, with the corset dangling off the end of his finger, "that someone threw discretion to the wind in here some night?"

Dozens of bags of rubbish and a collection of miscellaneous objects were dragged out of the woods. Then the local farmers with tractors and trailers brought them to a central point at the end of the village for collection by the council. In our parish the farming community with their machinery and expertise are a vital component in any undertaking. The coming together of all facets of the community is the lifeblood of any parish. On the last evening of the clean-up, hundreds of bags lined the roadside. Passing motorists slowed to view the array. One exhausted worker had taken time to place a large sign on top of the rubbish bags asking, "Is any of this rubbish yours?"

A week afterwards, when all the bags had gone, the grass was cut and everything was in pristine condition, a black bag of rubbish appeared on the same spot. The word went around the village like lightning. A crowd gathered. We could not believe our eyes! The strange thing was that before the big clean-up the same bag could have lain there for a week and nobody would have even noticed. But now we were on high alert. We investigated the bag and discovered that it belonged to a French woman who was renting a nearby house. She told us, "I see much rubbish so I think that is the place for it."

It was into the village and the approach roads that we put our greatest effort. Soon we had both sides of the main road into the village landscaped and looking well. But then the National Roads Authority (NRA) undertook roadworks that left it in the condition of a ploughed field. A large team of volunteers was rounded up to tackle the problem. After a few hours, one disgruntled man pronounced: "This is bloody slave labour. No voluntary group should be expected to do this." Another man who had arrived in his brand-new car finished up so caked in mud that he had to walk home to hose himself down and then come back for his car. A group of teenagers who had come to help for the first time went home covered in mud and after that experience we never again saw them. We went back to the NRA to demand that remedial work be carried out, but the NRA had subcontracted the job and so claimed not to be responsible. We then had a prolonged battle with various statutory bodies, and because we refused to go away we eventually got things put right.

The night before we were due to be judged for a "Pride of Place" competition, disaster struck. At the end of the village a motorist in a hurry forgot to round the barrack corner and shot straight across the road and down three steps, spinning four large flower tubs into the air and then ramming his engine under an ancient flower-filled farm cart. The resulting debris covered the entire corner in a carpet of battered flowers, earth and smashed tubs. It was testimony to the solidity of the old cart that it had refused to budge and remained unshaken by this modern monster rammed between its shafts. Our crazy motorist, meanwhile, had reversed out of the war zone and gone merrily on his way, unaware that he had disturbed the arm of the law in the barracks across the road, who went in hot pursuit.

The following morning, when the chaos was sighted, an SOS went around the village. We gathered to survey the scene. Speedy action was required, so we quickly got to work with brushes and wheelbarrows. New tubs and shrubs were procured and paid for by our speeding friend, and by lunchtime all was well. We were once more ready for inspection, and with new tubs and new shrubs we were better than ever. One of the nuns in our cookery class in school had always told us that the secret of success was to turn a kitchen disaster into a dinning-room triumph — a lesson to be applied to all walks of life!

In the fight against litter, Cork County Council set up the Litter League to select the cleanest town and village in the county. We struggled manfully to take the award, as the cash prize would help buy plants and trees. But keeping clean and tidy a village through which 30,000 vehicles pour daily is no mean task, and of course we also have our own litterers. My husband Gabriel was the stalwart of the litter-pickers and did a round of the village early every morning before taking in the post and beginning his day's work. During the day, others did shifts in the village and along the approach roads. Every morning, on my shift, I found an empty packet of a certain brand of cigarette in the same spot, and if it was missing, I wondered if the smoker was all right — there is a set pattern even to litter. The Celtic Tiger was to be met daily in our midst when we picked up unopened tins of beer and full bags of crisps.

Picking litter can have its funny side. One day, as I was going up the hill behind our house, a woman smoking a cigarette came towards me. Suddenly she waved her cigarette in the air and announced loudly: "Don't worry, I wouldn't throw a butt on the ground within a mile of Innishannon!" We had declared a public war on litter and the news had travelled even beyond the parish boundaries. A young girl very seriously told me, "I always threw my rubbish out the window of the car. I saw nothing wrong with it until the Litter League began. But now I take a bag around in the car for the rubbish." So at least we were creating awareness. In the first year of the competition we came second in the county, and in the second year we came first.

The Tidy Towns is a combination of slave labour, dogged determination and occasional diplomatic skill. One night after a particularly depressing meeting I discovered that another component was necessary. The night in question, as we walked up to the annual meeting in the parish hall, I felt that this was going to be a great meeting. We had enjoyed our best year to date, having won the National Landscape Award and come first in the Litter League. But I was in for a rude awakening. One member started to *cnáimhseáil*. This in English means whining, but the English word only half conveys the meaning. There are some occasions when we have to resort to the native tongue to convey true clarity of meaning.

The strange thing about a meeting is that, if it takes off in one direction, it is very difficult to turn it around. The sheep element in us comes to the surface and we all follow the leader out the gate. But on this occasion it was down a moaning road. By the time the meeting was over, I felt like lying down under the table and crying. We came home, Gabriel having taken it all in his stride, but I was grinding my teeth with frustration. I sat in the kitchen, simmering with bad temper. Mike, our eldest son, who unlike his mother never uses two words where one will do, breezed in and stopped dead in his tracks when he saw my face.

"What's wrong with you?" he demanded.

"I'm fed up with bloody Tidy Towns," I snapped.

"But you're the one with the big dream of beautiful Innishannon," he protested.

"Not tonight," I told him grimly.

"So the dream is after getting a bit of a rattling," he said, with a grin.

"It's dead!" I declared. "Dead, dead, dead."

There was a thoughtful silence and then Mike pronounced: "If you have a dream," he began slowly, "you must put that dream on the very top of the goalpost and play above the shit."

Our bridge at the western end of the village was shrouded in a thousand shades of mud and dust. It sorely needed a new coat, but first it would have to be washed, which would necessitate getting a tractor — or preferably two — with power hoses on to the bridge to give it a good wash. The problem was the traffic that thundered relentlessly over the bridge. To avoid causalities, we would have to plan the entire enterprise like a military manoeuvre. It was decided that the early hours of a Sunday morning would be the quietest time. But that would not apply if there was a big game on in Thurles, Croke Park or any up-country venue; if that was the case, every GAA supporter from Beara to Bandon would be on the road. So, after consultation with all sporting bodies, we chose our morning carefully. It was decided we would commence operations at 4a.m. on a Sunday in August. Two reliable farmers, Paddy and Ted, would bring their tractors, water tanks and power hoses, and Donal, our local garda, would take care of traffic. We would round up the usual slaves!

That morning, as I walked up the village at four o'clock, the dawn was breaking and I could hear the tractors already in action. As they moved along slowly, the workers behind were power-hosing down the iron rails of the bridge. It was a slow procedure as the rails were corroded with years of caked mud and grime. The

106

odd passing motorist slowed in amazement to see what on earth could be going on at that hour of the morning. Donal kept them informed and moving at the same time.

The lads worked in shifts and slowly the bridge came out from under its coat of dirt. To fortify the troops we had turned the stone wall at the far end of the bridge into a breakfast counter and dished out rashers and sausages with cups of tea. As we dined on our stone table it was lovely to see the rising sun send rays of light up the river and to watch the Bandon valley fill with light as the mist rolled along the top of Dromkeen Wood.

Early one evening the following week, a team of about thirty volunteers lined out with cans of paint. Some had never before wielded a paint brush but were there for the craic and finished up colour co-ordinated with the bridge, which before darkness fell glowed a burgundy red. One volunteer brought along an American visitor to help and she found it highly entertaining that a whole village was out painting a bridge. The project had been a marathon that was hugely enjoyed by the young, and on the next occasion that the bridge needed an overhaul the young farmers of the local Macra na Feirme club took it on board as their club project.

Tidy Towns is a testing organisation and there are occasions when you ask yourself why you bother, especially when you are out picking up other people's litter. You could be forgiven for thinking that it's a bit like trying to keep out the tide. But it stimulates pride in one's own place; friends meet up on a regular basis, and it gives newcomers an opportunity to get to know their neighbours and to integrate into their chosen community. If young couples come to live in our parish from places like Kenmare, Lismore or Clonakilty, they are a great asset as they have grown up with the pride-of-place ethos.

Over the years, many trees have been planted in the parish but the biggest planting project was the Millennium Grove — *Gort na Mílaoise*. As the millennium approached, we felt that there should be some permanent landmark on our landscape to record that big step in time. We appealed for sponsorship for trees, and the money came in freely from all over the parish in support of the project. Outside the village, by the side of the main road, was a long strip of waste ground that had become a dumping area. We hired machinery to have the ground cleared and levelled. Then we brought in loads of good topsoil to create a deep bed for the ball-rooted deciduous native trees that were going to move in and rest there for many years. In tree planting you get only one chance to give your young trees a rich, comfortable bed.

We went to the tree nursery of Matthew Neilson, just beyond our parish, and walked through acres of the most wonderful trees. It was a joy to see rows and rows of elegant native trees. A bit like children in a sweet shop, we were spoiled for choice, but with the help of Matthew, who is a wise and experienced tree man, decisions were finally made. The trees were delivered on the last Saturday of the last week of the last October of the old millennium. It was a damp autumn day. Almost the entire parish turned out for the occasion, bringing shovels and spades, and one man brought a digger. It took hours of digging and dragging the large trees into position before finally they were all standing. By then, we were wet, exhausted and covered in mud but so pleased with our efforts that we could have danced between the trees. Our priest and minister then blessed the grove.

There is nothing more conducive to the feel-good factor than planting even one tree. A whole grove of trees was a feast of delight. These trees would cleanse the air of the pollution from passing traffic and give homes to hosts of wildlife. Surely a blessed event.

CHAPTER
ELEVEN

The Kind Garden

"Did you ever think of opening your garden to the public?" D.J. of our nearby garden centre asked me.

"What!" I gasped. "My garden is not good enough to open to the public."

"Of course it is," he insisted. "All people want is just to see someone else's garden."

"D.J., I could never get my head around that," I protested.

"Well, think about it anyway," he told me. "You've an interesting garden."

If I had an interesting garden, it was not because of anything that I had done: it was simply that I had married into an interesting garden. Uncle Jacky had loved his garden and had created a peaceful haven that I had inherited. His garden had no set lay-out but had paths meandering through flower beds, drills of potatoes and rows of cabbage. His free-range hens scratched industriously wherever the inclination directed them, and our first beehive had sheltered under his apple tree. He would encourage anyone to be a gardener because he exuded his own love of it; his enthusiasm was infectious and he always had time to lean on his garden spade and have a leisurely chat. To me he was a real gardener because he grew food: he grew potatoes, vegetables, blackcurrants, gooseberries — in fact, almost all the food for Aunty Peg's kitchen table, and he kept us and some of the neighbours supplied as well. I loved Uncle Jacky and I loved his garden.

When he died, it grieved me to watch his garden grow into a wilderness. Gabriel and I were too bogged down with children and the family business to take care of it. But sometimes late in the evenings after work I would stand at the garden gate and say to the garden and Uncle Jacky: "Some day I will get out here and bring you back to your former glory." Gabriel kept the grass cut, but apart from that, the shrubs, plants and trees were left to their own devices. The boys had turned the lawn into a football pitch and the dogs thought that it was Shelbourne Park greyhound track. The daffodils and old roses alone survived the neglect, so in spring and summer we still had flowers for picking. In autumn we had a great crop of apples off the tree that Uncle Jacky had planted as a young man. People who plant trees leave a gift for the next generation and at Christmas time I was always grateful to him for his wonderful holly trees.

A garden behind your back door, no matter how neglected, is a blessing that enriches your house and kitchen table. It's a pity now to see gardens being sold off as sites for second houses and neither house finishes up with a garden. We need gardens to nourish our souls and give us breathing space from each other, and to give children a place to play and let off steam. It is not outside the realms of possibility that in the future houses will be removed to give people back green spaces.

In the end, it was a strange twist of fate that led me back out into my neglected garden. A retired lady who lived down the river had come to stay with us as she recovered from the death of her husband. It started off as a temporary arrangement, but she stayed with us until she died fourteen years later. The day after her funeral, my sister Frances rang from Kent to find out how we were. I told her that we were somewhat *trína chéile*, and she instructed me to go out and plant a tub in the backyard. Planting, she told me, was good therapy. I did as I was told; one tub led to another, and I discovered that she was right.

Our collie dog, Lady, also found the tubs beneficial, and each night she slept in a different one. Every morning I raged at her beside my tub of flattened flowers. Lady crouched on the ground and covered her head with her two paws and curled up in a ball of mortification. But her act of contrition was not followed by any firm purpose of amendment, and that night she repeated the performance. So I extended my activity into the garden where there was more space, but Lady's counter-activity continued, and whereas I was on my own, she had her companion Bran to assist her in the nightly uprooting.

Despite Bran and Lady's efforts I persisted and, if I complained to my sister Phil about the dogs, I was told without sympathy that dogs and gardening did not go

112

together. So, undaunted by canine opposition and football damage, I succumbed to the lure of the garden and discovered that after a day spent there I could dance with happiness. The whole population of Innishannon, it seemed to me then, was perfect, whereas if I had spent the day doing our shop accounts, I could eat thorny wire and snap the nose off anyone who crossed my path. Gardening, I had discovered, was a mental massage.

I became very fussy about garden edging, much to the amusement of Gabriel who protested, "I've cut the grass out here for years and never heard a word about edging, and now all of a sudden it's all about edging."

As the years went by, the footballers outgrew the lawn and Lady and Bran went to the burial plot in the grove at the top of the garden. But it was when our friend Con died that I discovered the true value of gardening. He died in January and the following weeks and months I spent working in the garden. Hours of digging eased the pain of grief. It was as if the pain was absorbed into the brown earth. It made me realise that we are deeply connected to the earth and that nature is a powerful silent healer.

So a deep love affair developed between me and Jacky's garden. I felt that he had left behind him a patch of sacred ground. Though I was full of enthusiasm, I had very little gardening knowledge but became an avid garden-book and magazine reader, and every Saturday I went straight to Charlie Wilkins' column in the *Irish Examiner*. Margaret Griffin from

Dripsey Garden Centre came and set me on the right road, and from there on it was a case of trial and error.

Gabriel and I worked out there together: he was the greenkeeper and I was the plants woman. We had defined demarcation lines: the lawns were his and the beds were mine. There was good reason for this strategy as a few years previously I had asked Gabriel to weed Jacky's grave, which I had turned into a wild flower garden. When I went to see it that evening, the grave was as clean as a whistle with not a flower to be seen.

"What did you do?" I wailed.

"Well, you said to clean it," he protested.

"But, but . . ." I began.

"Well, I won't get that job again," he said with a grin. He didn't!

Together we had great days in the garden, and unless it was raining or freezing, we had our lunch out there and the birds got so accustomed to this that they gathered around the table to be fed. The blackbirds became so cheeky that one of them would come on to the table for the crumbs, and if you happened to bring out the tray and had to return to the kitchen, leaving it unattended, the blackbirds had a head start. They had decided that this was their place and it always surprised me that a blackbird could attack and chase away the much bigger crow. But they also bullied the gentler thrushes, who were not as brave, and only when the blackbirds were absent did the thrushes venture out from beneath the hedges. We had put nesting boxes along the high stone garden wall, and one day it amused me to watch a blue tit go from box to box on a tour of inspection. He was house-hunting and not prepared to settle for any old house. At the top of the garden stands the old stone Methodist preaching hall, and the birds burrowed in between the large stones to build their nests; as they flew back and forth, they would put you in mind of a high rise apartment for birds.

We seemed to spend more time in the garden than in the house, and when friends called they invariably finished up in the garden. We were out there when 9/11 happened. Lena, who was home on holidays, got a text from one of her friends in Boston and we came into the house to watch the tragedy unfold.

If there was any upset in our lives, I invariably gravitated to the garden, where I could sit quietly and recover. Gabriel had given me a birthday gift of a garden diary, beautifully illustrated with quotes and flowers, and I had decided to keep it for recording happy garden thoughts and to write in it only in the garden. So the garden was my healer and comforter, and though I had protested to D.J. that I did not consider my garden good enough to open to the public, there was another factor also at the back of my mind. This was my special place: did I really want to open it to the public? The other side of the equation was that from my garden I could look up at the church steeple which was now wrapped in scaffolding. Refusing to help would be akin to refusing to support a friend with his head enclosed in plaster.

Gabriel had no problem with opening the garden, but then he was always more generous than I was. It was one of the traits that I always loved in him and my miserable side was the element that I liked least about myself. For a few days I struggled with my decision and in the end came down on the side of opening. After all, I concluded, it would require far less work than the other fundraisers for the church. That's what I thought!

Opening your garden to the public makes you view it in a whole new light. Trojan work is required to bring it up to what you would consider the necessary standard. You could not expect people to come and pay to look at a wilderness. I knew from the experience of garden visiting that gardeners hope to see something different and learn something new. The first garden I had ever visited was that of Brian Cross. That was back in the days of football and dogs in my garden. When I came home, I looked askance at my own wilderness. But that visit gave me motivation, and though I would never achieve Brian Cross's perfection, it still got me going and in later years, when I revisited his garden, I came home less depressed by my own.

So began the big effort to dig and prune. Plants that had grown too tall for the front of the border suddenly found themselves demoted to the back benches. Colour co-ordination became a big issue and I began to view my garden as a palette of colour for an oil painting, though I soon discovered that I was no Monet or Mildred Ann Butler. About a week before the opening, I viewed a bed around the base of the elegant silver birch with a critical eye. I began an extensive overhaul and when the whole place resembled a demolition site my young friend Henry called in and viewed it with a jaundiced eye.

"Alice, are you sure that you're not going backwards?" he wanted to know. As well he might! But by evening all was well and the Johnson's blue that had lost the run of themselves at the front of the bed were now firmly put in their place in the back row. Some plants, like people, have no manners and would walk all over others if they got away with it. But Henry's comment had put a stop to my gallop and I decided that I would have to refrain from the big dig.

As luck would have it, I had to go into Cork for a book signing the day before the opening, but all was in readiness — or so I thought. When I came home, my sister Resa was installed in the backyard, surrounded by chaos. The whole place was in disarray as she shifted tubs while water and earth were gushing all over the yard.

"What are you doing?" I cried in dismay.

"This place is too itty bitty," she declared, rolling a big tub down the yard.

"But Reeees..." I began in protest, but her daughter, my beloved niece Eileen, interjected.

"Alice, come in and we'll have a cup of tea."

Inside in the kitchen, over a cup of tea, I regained my equilibrium. We came out and joined Resa in her major overhaul, and when it was done we were all in a state of exhaustion. But the yard did look better.

The previous week I had got a phone call from Ann Cronin, whose son Don is a sculptor living in the parish. She offered a collection of plants for sale, and

117

when they arrived I found that they were very unusual but were all labelled with names and planting instructions. Gardeners love unusual plants at open gardens and she had given us dozens that she had grown herself; I knew the visitors would be delighted with them. In addition, we received raffle prizes from the local garden centres, whose owners were all unstinting in their support.

Before we opened on Saturday morning, Gabriel and I walked around the garden; I felt so proud of it and sensed in my bones that Uncle Jacky would be glad that his garden was looking so well, and opening to make money for the church where he had prayed all his life and beside which he and Aunty Peg now rested. We had put up information details on the interesting points of the garden: the story of the old Wesleyan hall; the site of the village well, and the Churchill path. Winston Churchill's aunt, Clara Jerome, was married to a Frewen who had previously owned the land behind our house, and down through our garden was a path to the river which Churchill used when he went fishing while staying with his aunt. My favourite corner of the garden was Jacky's apple tree that provided an umbrella beneath which you could shelter on warm days to read, write or eat.

Over the years, I had collected pieces of statuary, and my favourite was a Portland stone statue of St Joseph that I had acquired from Glencommeragh, a house belonging to the Rosminians. I was looking for a St Francis of Assisi because with his love of birds he would be ideal for the garden. I had asked Fr Jimmy

Brown of Glencommeragh about the possibility of getting a St Francis, but Fr Jimmy had told me that he had none. He asked would I instead settle for Joseph as he was behind the back door waiting for a good home. So, one day we had gone back up to Glencommeragh and brought home Joseph, which was a major undertaking as he was a ferocious weight. On getting him home, our first job had been to strip off his coat of white paint to expose his natural stone, and within a few years he had lost his ghostly white appearance and mellowed into the garden.

My favourite piece of garden furniture was an iron chair made out of horseshoes by a friend of Billy the Blacksmith after Billy had died. Apart from the garden itself, all these bits and pieces added interest to the walk about it.

We were to open from 10 a.m. to 6 p.m. on Saturday and Sunday, and we needed to have two people on the gate and two on the raffle table, plus a change of shift every two hours. So, it was a case of "round up the usual suspects". In every parish you have great people who are willing and able to help out in all situations. They provide the teamwork that keeps the lifeblood pulsing through the veins of any community. The helpers lined up and changed shifts and had great fun between themselves and with the visitors. Even when their turn was over, they walked around the garden, chatting with friends and neighbours. Some people are so generous they would do your heart good.

As soon as we opened the gate, people began to come in and you could soon pick out the gardeners from the people who were just out for the day. The gardeners began just inside the gate and went slowly around the entire garden and wanted to know about different flowers and plants. I must say that I learned more from them than they did from me, because most of these gardeners had years of experience whereas I was a recent convert, and like all converts I was full of enthusiasm but possessed little knowledge. Around the garden we had placed large baskets of fresh fruit, so people were able to indulge as they went along.

It was interesting to watch the gardening fraternity. There were mothers and daughters both equally interested; mothers-in-law and daughters-in-law who had formed a common bond; couples young and old with both of them into gardening; and other couples where one — usually the man — was just dragged along. But some men were deeply interested and this was the case with one who walked with me around the garden and introduced me to some of my own plants. When we came to one corner to which I had given the "bum's rush", he surveyed it sadly.

"Ah! you could have done a bit better there now," he protested. He was right, and he said it in such a kindly way that there was no room for offence.

Another man who had obviously been dragged in by his wife walked around at first looking a bit uneasy. Then he met some of his neighbours and settled down. When I encountered him strolling around a few hours later, he told me, "This is a grand place you have here, a bit like a haggard."

120

One lady was heard remarking to her companion as she left, "Yerra, mine own place is just as good. Sure there isn't head nor tail to this place."

Uncle Jacky, I thought, would have loved that comment.

Saturday was a busy day but nothing compared to Sunday when the people absolutely poured in; at one stage, you could not see the garden for people. Prior to opening, one of the things that had worried me was how the birds would react to this intrusion into their privacy. The blue tits, after an initial fluttering of wings and a bit of circling like planes over Heathrow, decided that they would have to make a dive for it. They grew more confident as time progressed, and, by the end of the day, they were totally ignoring the people. The robins up in the grove, however, had a different reaction. They flew around in annoyance and when some of the children decided that the steps up one side and down the other side of the grove provided an area for them to run through, the robins went berserk. They screeched and flapped around in anger, so much so that one woman said to me in dismay, "Those robins will attack someone."

Carla Blake, the *Irish Examiner* columnist, who happened to be in the garden at the time, took me aside and said quietly, "Put up a sign on the steps of the grove: 'No entry — Birds nesting'."

I did as this wise woman told me and the robins calmed down, having got their grove back.

It was a very sociable event, and the fact that it was a lovely sunny day added to the enjoyment. People were able to stand and chat, exchanging gardening ideas. Some visitors enjoyed themselves so well that they stayed for hours. But one visitor went home with more than happy memories. I had very carelessly forgotten to take in my Felco pruner off the back windowsill, only to find afterwards that it had "walked". It had been a birthday present from Gabriel about which we had had a lot of laughs because he was surprised that a pruner could cost so much. It was the sentimental attachment that I had for the pruner that made the loss so hurtful. So if you are reading this and you have my Felco pruner, please drop it back through my letterbox!

When we closed the gate after the last visitor, there was not a scrap of litter to be seen, which said a lot for the gardening fraternity. We all retreated to the kitchen and had tea and a post mortem. During those two days we had a lot of fun, but we had also made €6,000 for the church. Now I could look up at the steeple and not feel guilty!

CHAPTER
TWELVE

The Unveiling

For generations a fire had glowed in the forge at the western end of our village. As you pass over the bridge, leaving the village behind, the road branches right to Bandon and left to Kinsale; there, in the elbow of the junction, nestled the forge. Behind it rose the majestic trees of Dromkeen Wood where a stream tumbled down the slope into the Bandon river. It was a landmark on the road to West Cork and probably one of the last authentic forges in Ireland. People could see through the forge doorway the warm glow of the fire, and outside it the wiry figure of Billy, wearing his leather apron and tweed cap, bent over the hoof of a horse. But in 1992 Billy, our last blacksmith, died and with him went a whole way of life. The corner that had been alive with the sound of the anvil and the sight of prancing horses became a silent place.

On the hill behind the forge, peering down through the trees, rose the gaunt ruin of Corr Castle. Generations of village children had played in the ruins of this castle and we thought that eventually it would be left like so many other historical sites to fall down and disappear. But since he was a child Richard Good

Stephenson, whose ancestors had built the castle, had had a dream. He, too, had played in the ruins and had called to the forge where Billy had dried out his wet shoes with hot coals. In later life he had set up a restoration firm for old buildings in England where he gained much valuable expertise. He returned to Ireland with a skilled workforce and began restoring Corr Castle — a slow, painstaking procedure in which every original detail was preserved or recreated to bring the castle back to its former glory.

In the meanwhile, beneath Corr Castle the old forge nestled silently at the foot of the hill, and some of us hoped that Billy, who had worked there all his life, would be commemorated in some way. In addition to shoeing horses, Billy had fixed children's tricycles and wheelbarrows, and the forge had been a waiting point for the bus and a meeting place for everybody. His forge provided a social centre for farmers and members of the racing fraternity, and all aspects of the horse world were discussed in there. Billy was also an enthusiast for greyhounds and was part of the large greyhound racing group in the parish. As he knew so much about the seed, breed and generation of local families, the forge had been a centre of genealogical enquiry and one of the focal points of parish life. Now it was gone, but many felt that it would be good to have it remembered in some way. It soon struck us that a sculpture of a blacksmith was the obvious choice.

Fate stepped in when a well-known sculptor came to live in the parish. Don Cronin had among his many creations the bull in Macroom, Eamon Kelly in Kerry,

Sarah Curran in Newmarket and Hanna Sheehy-Skeffington in Kanturk. To have him living in our parish put wings under the dream of a sculpture at the forge. At the same time, the National Roads Authority (NRA) was doing a big job on the main road through the village, and we thought that we would get funding through a scheme that provided for 1 per cent of the cost of public projects to go to appropriate arts initiatives. This would have helped wonderfully to finance a sculpture. However, we discovered to our great disappointment that we were mistaken in our hopes of the scheme. Nevertheless, by the time we discovered that we were mistaken, the idea of the sculpture had taken root. We had the sculptor and we had the site: all we needed was €25,000. We were so confident that we could raise the money that we told Don to begin work on the sculpture.

The main source of our finance would have to be the equestrian fraternity from all around the country. We hoped that they would see this as an opportunity to acknowledge the contribution of blacksmiths to the racing industry. It would be difficult to fundraise in the parish, where collections for the church were in full flight. Nevertheless, we let it be known that any contributions would be welcome. Billy had served the farmers and horse industry well, both within and outside the parish, and we hoped that it was not forgotten.

We set up a fund called "Friends of the Forge", which was initiated with €4,000 of *Candlelight* money. We applied for every grant we thought might be available and became expert at filling out forms. Then we wrote to all the top names in the horse industry; most of them came good, including one former taoiseach who sent us a cheque for €500; a big-hearted Dublin writer did likewise. Our single biggest donation came from a stables within the parish which donated €1,000. Families who had long associations with the forge joined together and pooled their donations, and two young brothers gave us €1,000 between them.

Fundraising is always full of surprises. Any day we received a good cheque in the post we were delighted, but when we got a polite suggestion that there were grants available for such things we did not feel so good. From some state bodies to which we had applied for grants we received polite suggestions of other more suitable departments to which we might apply. Eventually, Cork County Council came up trumps: first with a €2,000 grant and then we qualified under a European scheme for a grant of €12,000.

Richard Good Stephenson had begun to restore the forge building as a fitting background for the sculpture. Things were looking good.

Meanwhile, not far from the forge, Don was working on Billy. After a few months, Paddy, an old friend and neighbour of Billy's, and I were invited to go to view the work in progress. When we entered the workshop we gasped in amazement. Billy was standing there looking at us. It was uncanny. Don had captured the very essence of the man. He asked Paddy if he had got it right and, to his amusement, Paddy told him that Billy wore his cap further back on his head. The next step for Billy was to be brought to the foundry in Dublin to be bronzed. The next step for us was to work out a date for the unveiling.

Returning from a book signing on the mellow evening of the last Saturday in October, I decided to walk over to the forge to see how things were progressing. As I came across the bridge, an amazing sight met my eyes. Billy was suspended high above the forge on the tip of Liam Connolly's digger, and very slowly he was being lowered into position. On the ground, Don and Paddy were directing operations. Don had the positioning worked out to the last fraction of an inch, and with meticulous precision the sculpture was eased carefully onto a precise spot on the limestone plinth. Liam had the control of his huge machine so finely tuned that he could move chess pieces. Finally Billy, with his anvil and sledge, was back in his own place. At the forge corner a second dream was being realised.

During the week before the unveiling, the sculpture was wrapped in black plastic, and on Sunday morning we peeled it off and replaced it with an elegant red cloak. After all, nobody would come to a big event in black plastic, especially if you were the guest of honour. An hour before the unveiling, cars began to park all around the forge corner, down the Quay road, up Colony Hill and all along the village. But we had no confusion as Gabriel with a group of locals well accustomed to parking cars kept everything running smoothly. A huge crowd gathered around the restored forge. The guest speaker was an old friend of the family

127

and when a light shower began to sprinkle us he sought divine intervention and the rain stopped immediately. We were pretty impressed but it came as no surprise to Fr Power.

Billy's sister cut the ribbon, the red cloak flowed to the ground and Billy was revealed in all his detail. People gasped in amazement and then stood back and surveyed him. Some of the men walked around him as if they were buying a thoroughbred. There was unanimous agreement that it was perfect. When you put something up for public appraisal there is nearly always some know-all who thinks things should be better. On that day there were none — which was probably the third miracle at that corner!

CHAPTER
THIRTEEN

Quacking Time

Do you sometimes wake up in the morning feeling that you could put your head under the pillow and wish that the day would go away? Well, not so with our new residents who last year moved into the grotto at the end of the village. For years the grotto had just two saintly residents who lived in splendid isolation — the Blessed Virgin and St Bernadette. These two holy women had been brought there by Aunty Peg, who went into Neffs of Cork in the late 1950s and had them made to measure. An adjacent householder had given them a free site, and it was a perfect home for them because that end of our village, called The Rock, provides an ideal location for the Blessed Virgin, who from her high vantage point, a stream flowing at her feet, can overlook the village.

Every summer in the past, a procession of praying people came down the hill and along the village from St Mary's Church to fill the grotto with prayers and incense. Those were the days when the traffic through our village generated only a gentle hum and we could move easily between the occasional cars. The Celtic Tiger was just a cub then, but with the progress of years he grew into a formidable force. He took control of our roads and roared through our village; the faint hum of the occasional car accelerated into the thundering rumble of 30,000 vehicles per day. This rendered meandering devotional processions out of the question, and the grotto was no longer a place of pilgrimage.

Then something happened to change matters. Baby ducks were introduced to the grotto, which with its grassy slopes and flowing stream was an ideal location for them. It once again became a place of pilgrimage, as people come to feed the new residents. Now, instead of the sound of praying voices we had the quacking of ducks, and the wonderful smell of incense was replaced by the pungent odour of the duck house.

The ducks were a celebration of new life and they welcomed the day with an exuberance that was contagious. When you opened the duck-house door in the morning, the occupants quacked with delight and rushed out, spreading their wings, and ran across the grass, covering themselves in a shower of sparkling dew. Then they peered down into the stream with screeches of anticipation. They tumbled down the stony path, some of them head over heels, so overcome with excitement at the prospect of getting into the gurgling water. There they plunged and flapped with quacks of exhilaration. They swam up and down, twirling around like brown ballerinas. Sometimes they did head-stands and pushed their heads down into the depths, leaving only their bobbing tails above the surface. They seemed so happy to be alive! *Wouldn't it be wonderful*, I thought to myself, *if we were all as exuberant as the grotto ducks?* Just watching them would make you feel good.

The Blessed Virgin kept a motherly eye on them, and as they waddled around Bernadette she must surely have been glad of their presence because before she became a saint she was of peasant stock and probably grew up surrounded by wildlife. Now the ducks quacked around her brown-skirted kneeling figure. Their days were spent swimming up and down the stream, and then they came out to investigate the grassy slopes of the grotto for stray flies and slugs; when the search was over, they stretched out in the warm sun. When the rain came and caused us humans to complain, the ducks welcomed it with quacks of delight. Sometimes hot or cold will not please us humans but the ducks were accepting and happy for everything that might come their way.

The world of the wild duck is fraught with the danger of otters, mink, rats and foxes, but ducks live in the "now". It is as if they believe the story of the lilies in the field. However, their friends, John and James, did not share the same faith as the ducks so they wired the little bridge below the grotto because we thought that it was up from the river the mink would come to attack our ducks. It was a terrible tragedy for the wildlife of Ireland when, with the cessation of mink farming, these black demons were let loose along our rivers where they indiscriminately kill our native species. It is to be hoped that with the increase of the otter life along the rivers these merciless killers will be naturally overcome.

In the event, the killer did not come up from the river but one night came downstream and killed six of our ducks, taking two and leaving four dead bodies. So then we wired the upper end to prevent entry from above. To make doubly sure, we laid mink traps under the bridge and further upstream. We assumed that it was the mink who had somehow got in and wreaked havoc on our duck family, but a young lad who was passing late that night, hearing a hullabaloo inside the wall, looked in and chased away what he judged to be an otter. A man from Bandon fisheries assured us that it had the trade mark of a mink rather than an otter, but irrespective of what it was, keeping our duck family safe was proving to be a difficult task. The natural food chain is a very difficult one to put on hold, but for a few weeks our ducks were secure and the full number present and correct every morning.

Word of the grotto ducks spread around the parish and people came to visit; the ducks gratefully gobbled up any contribution that came their way. The children loved them.

Then one night a fox discovered that there was a new restaurant at the grotto, and after that he came nightly without any reservation. We were a duck less every morning. Our young ducks needed to be taken off the menu of this unwelcome visitor. We needed a secure home for our family. Happily the ducks were not victims of the property market, which has gone crazy around Innishannon. Our ducks had a free site in a prime location and the mortgage holders were Our Lady and Bernadette. The builders, John, James and

Paddy, came free, and Paddy brought the materials. In a matter of hours, the ducks had a secure refuge at the better end of town. It was made of wire and stakes, and after a week of rain a roof was added to try to maintain some measure of comfort.

Keeping a duck house dry and clean is a bit like trying to keep out the tide. Ducks are by nature messy and their webbed feet can turn a dry floor overnight into a brown pool. But at least they were safe as we put them in at night under the watchful eye of Our Lady and Bernadette. Now the fox could look but could not touch.

Then a problem arose that we had never anticipated: sex came to the grotto. It awoke in the young drakes and, as with all young and not so young, its discovery went to their heads and they absolutely lost the run of themselves. They wanted it for breakfast, dinner and supper. Part of the problem was that we had seven drakes and six ducks, so seven into six wouldn't go; demand exceeded supply and the drakes had to queue up.

One very wet February morning, when the grotto stream had turned into a roaring torrent, the ducks paraded along the high bank but sensed that below the waters were dangerous and did not attempt to fly in or scramble down the path. However, one fool of a drake with only one thing on his mind chased a duck and, in her efforts to escape from his advances, she fell headlong into the brown, gushing water. She was whipped downstream but before she reached the little bridge she collided with an island of stones and clambered on to it. Two fighting drakes had tumbled in after her, but the roaring waters soon cooled their ardour. They were swirled around, turned upside down and whirled along until they crashed into the base of the path. Grasping at tufts of grass and stones, they finally struggled up to safety.

The activities of these over-sexed drakes were making life a misery for all our ducks. We wondered about tying their legs loosely together to put a stop to their pursuit, but some caring citizen would probably report us to the ISPCA. We thought of capturing some of the drakes and taking them down to the Bandon river, and one helpful visitor even suggested that we should buy chastity belts for the drakes! But, as in the case of so many problems, it was solved by time. When the hatching instinct took over, the ducks led the drakes downstream. There they hatched along the banks of the river, and now we see them happily swimming under the bridge and along the river by Innishannon Hotel. Perhaps they regarded downriver as a step up the property ladder, and even in the duck world it was a case of location, location, location.

CHAPTER
FOURTEEN

An Enchanted Evening

Linda's sparkling tones vibrated down the phone. She has a wonderful singing voice and even in conversation her words dance with musical notes.

"You were looking for me," she said happily. "What can I do for you?"

"I thought that we might have a musical evening in aid of our church restoration," I told her hesitantly.

"Great!" she declared. "What had you in mind?"

"Well," I ventured slowly, trying to convey exactly what it was I had in mind, "we don't want Italian opera but neither do we want 'The Fields of Athenry' . . . but maybe something for people who like kind of middle-brow stuff like *South Pacific* or *Oklahoma*. There's a whole squad of people out there who are not being catered for, the middle-of-the-road ones. Am I making sense?"

"Perfectly! What you want is" — and she launched into song — " 'Some enchanted evening, you may see a stranger, you may see a stranger . . . ' Is that what you have in mind?"

"Exactly," I told her with delight, "and you've just given it a name, so we'll have 'An Enchanted Evening', and will you be the lead singer?"

"Of course," she said with enthusiasm, which did not surprise me because in all the time that I had known Linda "generous" was the one word that she always brought to mind.

"We'll need a male voice as well," I ventured.

"I know the perfect guy," she told me. "He's Paud and, hold on and I'll give you his number."

And so the idea for the Enchanted Evening took root. We had all worked hard at fundraising and it was time to have an evening of entertainment and relaxation; an evening that would raise our spirits and give the parish a night to remember.

Linda has a voice like an angel and had entertained in the Cork Opera House, the National Concert Hall and many other venues around the country. We had got to know each other when she became the publicist for Brandon Books. It was her first job but she was born for public relations and I watched her in awe one night after her first *Late Late Show* as she charmed her way around RTÉ. Later, one producer told me that she was the most efficient PR person he had ever encountered. If she said that something would be on your desk in the morning, then it was sure to be there. A beautiful girl with a generous soul and the voice of an angel — it did not seem fair that one person should be so gifted!

With Linda on board we were off to a great start. But we always bore in mind what Kay from a nearby flower shop had told us when we were organising our first event, the Festival of Flowers: "People can't come if they don't know about it, and when they come make

sure that there's something worthwhile there for them."
It was a recipe applicable to any fundraising event.

The first step towards the Enchanted Evening was to
secure a venue. At the time, we were attending mass in
the Church of Ireland church because our own church
had been taken over by the builders. We were happy in
Christ Church, which has wonderful stained-glass
windows, a magnificent organ and — more important
than anything else for this occasion — superb acoustics.
It would be the perfect venue. The rector and their
church body were delighted with the proposal, and so
the scene was set and the next step was to put together
an entire show. In this, Linda was fantastic, and she put
us in touch with a wonderful pianist and violinist, both
of whom were willing to come. So, all that remained
was a compère and a choir to lace the whole
performance together.

A member of Cork Airport Singers lived in the
parish, and her sister was the conductor and her father
the director. Running any parish event necessitates
quarrying parish resources, and after a few phone calls
the choir agreed to perform and we soon found that the
man in charge was a well-organised perfectionist with
whom it was a pleasure to work.

Now all that remained to be found was the compère.
Just outside the village lived Elmery Mawe, who taught
in the parish and presented the Arts Programme on
96FM every Sunday morning. Steeped in music as she
was, I knew that she would be the perfect hostess
because she possessed the style and panache to grace
any setting. We now had the ideal cast but had to make

137

sure that the setting was conducive to an atmospheric night, and most of all we needed a good sound system. It was the one thing all the artists had mentioned.

For many years in Innishannon we had had our own rector living at the western end of the village, but when Rev. Foster retired he was not replaced, and Christ Church was serviced from nearby Bandon. Later, a young couple moved into the rectory, and the Christmas following their arrival a big storm brought down some of the rectory trees. For a few months afterwards, a large monkey puzzle lay prone beside the rectory gate, and as time went by I wondered if the couple in the rectory would give it to us for Tidy Towns to create a feature outside the village. The problem was that I knew nothing about the newcomers and felt it would be a bit rich to knock on a stranger's door and ask them for their tree. So I decided to do a bit of research. In the course of my inquiries I discovered that one of my neighbours knew this young man's father and declared him to be a grand man. So far so good, but what about his mother? I needed more than half a family tree before I would feel comfortable knocking on his door, begging. But when I found out who his mother was I knew that I was home and dry. He was from a family steeped in music and dancing, and by a strange quirk of fate his uncle had stayed with us years earlier and got us out of a tight corner.

Some years before, one of our teenagers had been involved in the local GAA club and had talked some of the older members, including his father, into booking high-profile showbands for a carnival marquee. The cost of these showbands at the time seemed astronomical to a small rural club and was in danger of giving the entire Valley Rovers Club a collective heart attack. But the greatest worry was the sound system. Would the showband's powerful sound system blow the top off the marquee and could we end up in a silent black dug-out? An electrical genius called Mickey who was a friend of Gabriel's came to the rescue. He stayed with us for the week and every night was on duty in the marquee to make sure that Butch Moore, Pat McGeegan, and Colm Wilkinson were heard not only in the marquee but all over the village. The showbands were a huge success and Mickey had saved the village from a nervous breakdown. He was a smashing man and we all enjoyed the week that he had spent with us.

The man in the rectory was Mickey's nephew; his name was Mike and not only did he give us the tree but he offered to do anything he could to help in the parish. He had a sound and lighting company and, like his uncle, was a genius in his field. We approached him about our Enchanted Evening and not alone was he prepared to do the sound and special lighting effects but he also offered to floodlight the beautiful old stone church on the night. Generous and willing parishioners like Mike contribute greatly to the parochial pot. They keep it simmering because if we are all taking out and nobody putting in, the bottom eventually falls out of the pot.

We were now ready to advertise our Enchanted Evening, but first we had to decide on the price of the tickets. This resulted in long and heated debates between people of the opinion that we were too dear and people who were wondering if we were running a charitable organisation. Eventually a compromise was reached and we began our publicity drive; within a short time, the bookings began to pour in. Gabriel was our floor manager, who counted and recounted the seating capacity of church pews, which was a bit difficult without rear circumference knowledge. He arranged and rearranged the layout of borrowed school chairs to achieve the maximum of seating, bearing in mind as well the comfort of the audience.

The plan was to have the audience in candlelight, with Mike spotlighting the performers on the altar that was the temporary stage. We decided to make the colour theme of the night burgundy, which was the dominant colour in many of the stained-glass windows. We draped the sills of the deep windows in rich satin, which would glow beneath the candles in the midst of flowing flower arrangements. We begged and borrowed brass candlesticks and candelabras from around the parish and placed them along the aisles. The beautiful old wooden pulpit was edged with flowers and beneath it would stand the candle-lit baby grand piano. The entrance porch was to be softly lit and filled with flowers, to set the atmosphere for the people as they came into the main body of the church. Candlelight, soft music and the scent of flowers would have the effect of slowing people down and soothing them into a more appreciative frame of mind. We wanted people to have a night to look back on as one of the magic moments of their lives.

The evening of the concert was soft and mellow. As people came up the wide limestone steps of the church, they stopped to admire the recently placed urn overflowing with glowing spring flowers. The incoming audience had risen to the occasion, with the ladies in glamorous outfits and the men in suits. Not an anorak in sight! It was lovely to watch smiles of appreciation light up their faces as they came into the transformed church porch. When they opened the door into the main body they gasped with delight to see the beautiful old church softly lit with candlelight and decorated with flowers. Mike had the altar area bathed in a warm glow, and above it the stained-glass window, flood-lit from outside, stood out in all its magnificent colours.

Even before they were seated, the audience sensed that they were in for a special evening. Along the front of the pews we had placed trays of chocolates. Eventually every seat was taken and the queue at the door had disappeared. Suddenly Linda appeared before me in the back porch, resplendent in a golden dress.

"My God, Linda," I gasped in dismay. "I thought that you were up front for the opening."

"Relax," she said with a smile. "I'm going to come up from the back, singing."

As she made her dramatic entrance and came up the aisle, Linda's wonderful voice filled the church. She had the audience in the palm of her hand. Paud provided a strong and rousing contrast, and when they joined together in duet they held the listeners spellbound. The pure notes of the violinist drifted around the church. You could hear a pin drop. The

141

Airport Singers opened and closed each part of the recital, their choice of songs delighting the audience. On the baby grand piano our wonderful pianist effortlessly accompanied the singers, and at times they all came together in performance. Elmery, with her musical knowledge and perfect sense of timing, linked the entire recital together in a delightful presentation.

My door duty over, I had slipped in at the back and sat on the organ seat where I had a bird's eye view of the whole church. During the entire recital nobody stirred, as they were entranced by the performance, and you could sense the waves of appreciation rippling around the church.

When the show had come to an end, the tea team came out of the vestry with trays of drinks and goodies and the performers were able to relax and discuss the performance with each other and with the audience. Tea-time after any event is wind-down time. The audience and the players were all so enthused by the experience that they wanted to share their delight with each other. It really was an enchanted evening.

CHAPTER
FIFTEEN

Don't Change Anything!

The church was finished. Having moved out in January, we came back in October. We left dampness and dirt; we returned to brightness and light. All involved in this transformation had learned something in the process. Three groups had set out on the journey: the parish; the building and finance committees; the design team. We on the committees were piggy in the middle.

Our first lesson began with the front wall of the church: it was a beautiful old stone wall, but the experts claimed that it was responsible for some of the interior damp because in earlier days it had been plastered. They assured us that it was never intended to be bare-faced and that it would have to be re-plastered. We reluctantly agreed. When the plastering began, a few growls of protest were heard around the parish; we explained, but the parish was not quite convinced.

Our next hurdle was trees. In front of this gracious old church, like a dirty dribbler around a baby's neck, lay an ugly expanse of tarmacadam. We decided to soften its harshness with elegant beech trees. They would frame the church, and as they grew larger the lower branches could be trimmed and cars could park beneath them. When the trees appeared, there were more growls of protest: the five trees were taking up the space of five cars! Cars, it seemed, were now more important than trees. We were learning fast: don't dare change anything.

So far the committee and the design team had agreed. But when we moved inside the church we locked horns. New liturgy and old parish practices do not always dance happily together. After the Vatican Council, parish priests and bishops had lost their common sense and nobody had cried stop; old saints had tumbled off pedestals and altars had been carted away.

Now we had more new liturgy. Rome had looked at the sanctuary area of her churches and had decided that all tabernacles and sanctuary lamps should be moved. But Innishannon is a long way from Rome and what works in the Vatican did not necessarily suit our small church; we decided that we would not be moved. Our liturgist was a bit put out by our reluctance to adopt the new thinking but we stuck to our guns and the tabernacle stayed in the same place, and the sanctuary lamp was moved just a little sideways to give an unimpeded view of the beautiful stained-glass window on the back wall. We won that round but gave in on the statues. And, boys, o boys, did we live to regret it.

The baptismal font was another story. The new liturgy decreed that it should be placed inside the main door. Now, putting a baptismal font in the middle of the only aisle of a small country church is not a practical proposition. It would block coffins coming in and brides going out. The male brains of Rome are far removed from the practical reality of ordinary parish living. No woman would have come up with such a daft idea! She would have anticipated the possibility of coffins being upended as bearers had to co-ordinate a sideway swing, or an excited bride falling over an unexpected obstacle on her dash to the altar. The chances of photographers using it as a grandstand for the perfect picture were not outside the realms of possibility. We argued with the liturgist and verbal battles ensued. He explained the symbolism of the cleansing baptismal font at the entrance and we could understand where he was coming from; it was fine for the sweeping aisles of cathedrals but would be a major traffic hazard in our small church. Eventually logic won the day and the font was placed into a recess halfway up the aisle, in front of the confessional. There, families had ample space to gather around for baptisms.

The next struggle was over the floor. One expert wanted to dig up the terrazzo and insert under-floor heating. It would be a very expensive job but design teams are not overly concerned with expense, whereas we had to answer to the parish. That apart, this floor had a lot going for it. Its delicately coloured mosaic designed to the contours of our church was an example of the skill of the original craftsmen. It was in perfect condition and, as well as being easy to maintain, it was bright and clean-looking. The decision hung in the balance until one morning a stonemason whose opinion carried a lot of weight strode in the door and asserted authoritatively, "That's a grand floor: don't touch it." He saved the day. The floor was polished and now looks great.

One of the most delightful experiences in the whole process of renovation occurred when the front of the choir gallery was slowly stripped of its old coat. For years it had been painted a depressing brown with sludge-yellow panels. The day the old coat was removed, out came rich oak panelling. It was unbelievable that for years this wonderful wood had been hidden from view. Now it glowed in all its perfection right across the centre of the church. Its emergence completely transformed the view from the front door. In earlier years, the choir had performed from this gallery, until the ceiling fell in on top of them. Then they moved up beside the altar. After the restoration, they opted to stay put. Some parishioners thought that they should have gone back to the gallery from where they linked the congregation with the altar; others agreed that they should stay up front where there was unity between them and the altar.

The old sacristy had become a terrible dumping hole, but now, having been cleared of all its detritus, it was transformed into a comfortable prayer room. A glass arch now linked it to the sanctuary, which made it a pleasant place for the infirm and parents and toddlers to attend mass. It previously had one large PVC window facing north, with a bleak view. A rich stained-glass window of the Good Shepherd, designed in the style that was contemporary with the original church, was donated to replace this. For the back porch

146

two more stained-glass windows were donated, one depicting St John at his desk scripting "The angel of the Lord declared unto Mary" and a companion for the opposite wall illustrating this story.

The original plans called for a very impressive new confessional to be constructed to the left of the back door. But budgetary needs kept it in its original place, which in retrospect was much better. Sometimes it can be good to be on a budget. As well as that, confessionals are no longer deemed necessary as sins have gone out of fashion.

The elegant steeple was rebuilt and years of weeds and shrubs removed from between the cracks in its stone work. The magnificence of the wonderful arched ceiling was highlighted with subtle colour contrasts, while up-lighting raised your eyes in its direction. Our church was now a thing of beauty and a joy forever.

When all was complete, the official opening was presided over by our bishop, John Buckley, a West Cork bowler who had never lost the common touch. Many exclaimed with "Oohs" and "Ahs" as they entered the church. But one man was not impressed: "What did ye do with all our money?" he demanded. "Sure there's nothing changed."

Unfortunately one thing had been changed that we should have left alone. We had moved statues. Or to put it more correctly, we had not challenged the liturgical decision that they should be moved. Our Lady had gone from the sanctuary and had been raised to an elevated position in the choir gallery. From there she could look down over the church. The Sacred Heart

147

was now on a pedestal inside the main door, where he could watch the comings and goings. With outstretched arms he welcomed in his flock.

At first, there was no reaction to the moved statues, but then a gentle murmur came from the grassroots. It grew to a faint grumble and slowly swelled into an intermittent wail. Then it turned into a deafening roar. For a historical record, we had provided a leather-bound visitors' book inside the front door. We felt that it would be nice to have a record of parish visitors and, most of all, of returning immigrants. But it soon became a conduit for the statue protest and turned into a complaints manual. Trying to pour oil on troubled waters, Gabriel placed a halo on Our Lady. She might have been impressed, but not her supporters. The strange thing was that nobody worried about the poor Sacred Heart. It seemed that he could have emigrated and nobody would have cared, but his mother's move was upsetting half the parish.

Then Our Lady decided to take action. One night, she climbed down over the gallery, went straight up the church, and took up her old position to the right of the tabernacle She called to her son and heir to come back up to his rightful place. When he arrived, she sent for St Joseph and told him to go down and mind the main door. After all, Joseph was the man of the house and it was his job to welcome in the visitors. Then peace reigned.

It was great to have the job done, but we were only halfway there because we had another church in the northern side of the parish which was in a worse state than St Mary's and was awaiting restoration. The parish had been divided by the West Cork railway line: Knockavilla lay to the north and Innishannon to the south. It created an artificial border in the parish and introduced a north-south mentality. The railway closed in 1962 but the division was still in the mental geography of some parishioners. The fundraising, however, was intended for both churches and embraced the entire parish, which was very good for cross-border relations.

Having just finished one church restoration, facing into another was a daunting prospect. Then God decided to give us a break. A wealthy and generous parishioner donated a million. It was a mighty boost to our fundraising. We were delighted for ourselves but also for Fr Kingston, who had bent over backwards to keep us all happy. That he had succeeded was a bigger miracle than the moving statues!

CHAPTER
SIXTEEN

The Parish on Canvas

"Will I ever be ready?" she asked.

"Sure, of course you'll be ready," I assured her.

"I'm not so sure," she said doubtfully.

"What you need is a deadline," I suggested. "You've been talking about this art exhibition for the past few years but you're getting no nearer to it. When exactly had you in mind?"

"When I'm ready," she told me.

"But when will that be?" I persisted.

"Well, I'm not sure," she said vaguely.

"What are you waiting for?"

"I'm waiting for the right time," she asserted.

"I have a suggestion," I said hopefully. "Next year, Cork is European Capital of Culture. There's as much culture in Innishannon as Cork. So next year could be your year."

"That's not a bad idea," she agreed slowly, and I sensed that she was considering it seriously. But then she had second thoughts. "Would I ever be ready?"

"Sure, of course you'll be ready," I assured her; "you've a whole year and a half and you already have paintings. Not enough, but once you're focused you'll get there."

"It's probably a good year to do it," she said thoughtfully, and I could see that the idea was beginning to take hold. As we drove home, we discussed the entire project, and by the time we reached Innishannon, the decision had been made. She had one whole year to get ready.

"Michelangelo did a big patch of the Sistine Chapel in that much time," I told her.

"I'm no Michelangelo," she said with a laugh.

Years previously, Mary and I had both started painting with Lia Walsh, who after the parish history exhibition started an art class in the village hall. When Lia no longer held classes, we joined up with Brother Albert in Cork, who patiently over the years tried to turn us into artists. Mary is the more talented of us, and many local people had come to her to do paintings for them. Now it was time to spread her wings, and an exhibition was the way to go.

The first decision to be made was the venue and, after much discussion, it was decided that the parish hall was the best place. Easily accessible to locals, it had the advantage of being on the side of the main road to West Cork; even though we were always complaining about the through traffic, on this occasion it could serve our purpose.

During that summer, autumn and winter, Mary painted and painted. She loves her own place and that love found expression in beautiful scenes of Innishannon. A great walker of Dromkeen Wood, which lies at her back door, she would have seen it in all seasons and at every hour of the day and night. Now these woodland observations poured on to the canvas in the shapes of pheasants flying over the wood in the early morning and the waterfall glistening in the evening light. Dromkeen in spring is a bluebell wood and in summer a place of light and shade. Mary's paintings brought the viewer into her wood in all seasons.

The parish hall needed a bit of an overhaul for an art exhibition. Con Dan, a builder neighbour of Mary's, came to the rescue and, with Mary's husband Joe, created the more intimate space of an art gallery. To the left of the door we planned long tables for wine and eats and, to the right, seating where five local teenagers would provide soft classical music on violin and harp. A neighbour who worked with a wine company would take care of the wine. When we discussed the eats, Lena, who was home on holidays from America, surprised me by assuring us that she would take charge of that department. She was then working in the financial world in Boston and told us that she knew exactly what was required for such an occasion. But I was apprehensive about her one-woman catering effort.

Dromkeen Wood on the morning of the exhibition was a carpet of bluebells spreading from under the trees into Mary's garden. She came into the parish hall with arrangements of primroses and bluebells. They filled the hall with their woodland scent and highlighted the paintings of bluebells and ditches of wild flowers waiting to be hung. All day, Mary, Ellen and I, ably assisted by Joe, hung the paintings. Hanging an exhibition is a challenging and exhilarating exercise; as the paintings went up, the wonderful beauty of Innishannon spread out around us.

Suddenly we realised that we had been so engrossed that we had forgotten to eat and time was running out. But before we left the hall we stood at the door to admire the entire scene. Mary and Joe went home to eat and get ready, while Ellen and I walked down the village looking forward to a cup of tea and to putting our feet up. We were exhausted! But when we opened the kitchen door we gasped in horror. Lena had every available space covered with dishes, trays, bowls and all kinds of everything.

"Have I the two of you for the rest of the evening?" she gasped in the relieved tones of a drowning woman. Ellen and I looked at each other in mutual dismay. No resting time to be had here!

"Where's your father?" I asked, seeking temporary relief.

"Evicted to the front room," she informed us, and there we found Gabriel calmly reading the paper.

"That kitchen is a war zone," he said with a smile and added, rising to the rescue, "You two look in the need of a cup of tea."

After tea, Lena issued instructions and the two assistants did as we were told. She had created little bits and pieces that I could not even christen not to mind guess what was in them. But potato skins I did recognise — after all, I had been reared on spuds.

"What the hell are you doing with potato skins?" I demanded.

153

"They are now a delicacy," she blithely informed me.

"Well, they might well be in downtown Boston, but some of tonight's clientele will be West Cork farmers," I protested. "Here we still regard potato skins as something that you give the dog after the dinner."

"Mother, you're caught in a time warp," she dismissively informed me. That's America for you!

When all was in readiness, I had to admit that the display looked good, including the potato skins, though I still had my reservations about them.

Mary's now-retired boss, Dr John Crowley, who had laid the foundation stones for the very successful SWS group where Mary worked, performed the official opening. All her fellow workers and the people of the parish came in strength. She was taken by surprise when Paudie from the local GAA club — for which Mary had done an immensity of secretarial work — presented her with a wonderful bouquet. She had also done major work for Tidy Towns and, when we presented her with a tree, one wit behind me commented, "That's a great present for someone living in a wood!"

People wandered around expressing "Oohs" and "Aahs" of delight as they recognised familiar scenes and, of course, we had the people who were interested only in the prices and meeting the neighbours. Early in the night, a young man had bought a painting of a local cottage as a surprise for his mother. Later, when she arrived in the hall, she was very disappointed to see the red dot, as she had wanted to buy this picture of her old family home. There were smiles all round when she discovered that he had bought it for her.

The night was an outstanding success and by the end of it the paintings were speckled with red dots. The eats had gone down a treat — even the potato skins; I had underestimated the farmers of West Cork.

CHAPTER
SEVENTEEN

The Day After an Ordinary Day

It was an ordinary day. On that Wednesday morning, after a leisurely breakfast, I went up to the attic to put foxes on canvas, and Gabriel went for his usual walk. He was a six-mile walker; I was only a three-miler and after the second mile I was thinking of all that I could be doing in the garden or up in the attic. Every morning, Gabriel got up before seven o'clock, and usually when I woke around eight he already had the shop open and had taken in the papers; when Mike came on duty, he went to mass and after breakfast usually had some project on hand.

Whatever direction either of us took after breakfast, we were both back in the kitchen by lunchtime, and when I came in the door Gabriel had the kettle on the Aga and was usually making sandwiches. Before he gave me the present of a laptop, I did all my writing up in the attic and, if I forgot to come down for lunch, Gabriel would appear with a tray and we'd eat up there, looking out over Dromkeen Wood. If we were both in the kitchen, Gabriel would always ask, "Are we inside or outside today?"

On that Wednesday, it was the usual question, and as there was a November chill in the air we opted for the front room that Gabriel had christened the curiosity room because from it you could watch the world of the village go by. My sister Ellen, who was staying with us at the time, had gone to Cork.

After lunch, Gabriel decided that he would like to see the plans for Knockavilla Church, the second church in the parish, which was about to be restored. The plans had been put on display in that church the previous Sunday. We drove up to Knockavilla and he viewed the plans with great interest, and because plans to me are a foreign language he pointed out different facets of the development. That night, there was a meeting in Knockavilla concerning the restoration and, because Gabriel was more meeting-friendly than I am, he opted to go and I locked up the shop as Mike was late home. When Gabriel came back from the meeting, he totalled the tills and then we had tea and discussed the meeting, and we went to bed still discussing the meeting.

The following morning, the bedroom door burst open and an ashen-faced Mike gasped:"Something's happened to Dad!"

I shot out of bed and, dragging on my clothes, tore down the stairs to the shop. Gabriel was on the floor with Dr Máire, who lives down the street, kneeling beside him. He was unconscious and she was setting up oxygen, and I crouched beside him with terror clutching my heart. Our neighbours, Declan and Shelly, were there, and Gerry who lives down the street was advising customers not to come in and explaining what was happening. Very soon, the ambulance was outside and the men brought in the stretcher; it was mind-numbing to watch Gabriel being carried out the door. Ellen and I climbed into the ambulance and, with siren sounding, we were on our way to the University Hospital. I felt that this could not be happening.

We were whisked into A&E where the medics took over and Gabriel was set up in a cubicle with drips and tubes. It was good to have Ellen because, being a nurse, she understood procedures, and as well as that she was calm and soothing. We sat by the bed as nurses and doctors came and went, but Gabriel remained unconscious. Gearóid came and we discussed what to do and decided that he should contact Diarmuid and ring Lena and Seán and tell them to book flights.

The day dragged on and nothing changed; late that evening, Gabriel was moved upstairs into a ward that had some very sick people. Through the long night, Lena, who had arrived earlier, and I sat with him as he remained in a coma, breathing quietly. The nurses were kind and comforting and brought us tea as the night crawled on. Because Gabriel's bed was by the window we saw the dawn break over Wilton. The next day dragged by and we sat with Gabriel, who showed no signs of regaining consciousness.

In the early hours of Saturday morning, I went down to the hospital chapel while the nurses attended to him. It was quiet and peaceful in the empty chapel. I tried to meditate and not let my mind run ahead of me but failed. What were we facing? Was it recovery or was Gabriel going to slip away from us? The thought of life without Gabriel's warm presence was a bleak prospect.

Then Lena tiptoed in, saying that the doctor wanted to talk with us. It could mean only one thing. Fear clutched my heart. The nurse directed us into a little office down the corridor from Gabriel's ward where the doctor was waiting. He was kind and gentle but his news was otherwise. Gabriel's condition was deteriorating and it was only a matter of time, and he emphasised that the time would be short. Lena, who was more alert than I was, asked for a private room.

They moved Gabriel into a little room, so now we could sit around his bed without disturbing anybody, which was not possible in the busy ward. During that long day, we prayed, we talked and we cried. Gabriel lay silent in the midst of us. He had great devotion to the rosary and now the praying of it had a calming effect on us. Time stood still and the world outside ceased to exist. Then, in the early hours of Sunday morning, he slipped away. In the presence of death you are made aware that life is beyond all understanding. It is a time when you switch to auto-pilot because otherwise you could not function.

The undertaker was contacted and I had thought that, as when Con died, he would come into the hospital and do what was necessary and that we could bring Gabriel home with us. But this was a different hospital and procedures had changed. Hughie the undertaker patiently explained all this to me on the phone in

159

great detail, and in the end I had to accept that we would have to go home alone. It was heartbreaking to walk out of that hospital and leave Gabriel behind. It was a bleak journey home.

We sat for a little while by the fire in the *seomra ciúin* and then it was time to go and pick out the coffin. Gabriel would have done this for me and he would have wanted something very simple. At the funeral parlour, Hughie was waiting and with great kindness walked us through rows of coffins. Because I was disorientated from shock and lack of sleep I saw coffins floating in the air around me and even Hughie, a fairly substantial man, seemed to take off into the air. I had to keep shaking my head to get back in focus, and eventually Gearóid and I picked out a plain coffin.

A few hours later, we were at the viaduct, a landmark with ample parking, waiting for the hearse, and when it drew up beside us it was mind-jerking to think that Gabriel was now inside in that coffin. We followed the hearse home to the village. Because eleven o'clock mass was on in the church there was parking in front of our own door. Gearóid and Diarmuid took in his coffin and placed it in the same spot where our friend Con's had been four years before. When the lid was removed, Gabriel looked so peaceful. He was dressed in his best suit, wearing his fáinne, his pioneer pin and his GAA tie of which he was so proud. We lit the wax candles in the old brass candlesticks around him. They were Aunty Peg's candlesticks and had gone around the village in her time to all the different wakes. They had been used at her own wake and at Con's and the feel of them was strangely comforting. It was so good just to have Gabriel with us.

For a little longer the final parting was put on hold and our minds were getting time to absorb this overwhelming reality. It was good then to be part of a small village community because they put their arms around us and walked with us every step of the way. Friends and neighbours poured into the house and throughout the day the extended family gathered. We cried and talked and comforted each other. All kinds of cakes and eats came in the back door and our friends Eileen, Noreen and Hazel took over in the kitchen; Ann, who lives across the road, brought a big pot of soup. Many times during that day, I thought that I was part of something that could not really be happening. But then I looked in at Gabriel in the coffin and knew that this was real. Late that night, some of us went to bed for a little while and the neighbours sat with Gabriel. Through the night, they talked, made tea and told stories beside him.

The following day, people came from further afield. His GAA and bridge friends gathered and many games were replayed in corners around the room. It was as if the full story of Gabriel's life was being woven around him. Bertie Kelleher, who had lived in our village for many years and was an exemplary member of the Garda in nearby Bandon, said something that stayed with me.

"In all the places I have served," he told me, "I have found in many cases that one solid citizen can hold an entire community together." It was the creed of the

Blasket islanders — *Ar scáth a chéile a mhaireann na daoine* ("We live in the shelter of each other.") Now, as a family, we were benefiting from that shelter.

During that day we sorted out readings and hymns. Con's brother, Fr Denis, was in America and we were unable to make contact, but his brother, Fr Pat from Clonard in Belfast, was with us, and our own priest, Fr John, who had been away on holidays, had miraculously appeared. Over the Christmas of Con's death, Gabriel had given Fr Pat a revised copy of Dinneen's Irish dictionary and had gone over with him the prayers of an Irish mass. In a strange twist of fate, now Fr Pat was going to say the mass in Irish. Gabriel would have wanted his funeral mass in his native language.

The time of the removal drew near and the house was thronged; among those present were many young people who over the years had done holiday work in the shop. I had never quite realised until then how many young girls had had summer jobs with us, and Gabriel and themselves had often had innocent fun together. Now they laughed and cried as they recalled some of the incidents that are part of running a local shop. As a teenager, Gabriel had delivered telegrams to remote corners of the parish where he had forged friendships with many families, and in more recent times, through sorting the mail, he was often the first to become aware of newcomers' addresses and to welcome them to the parish. For the new residents his was a welcoming face gone, and for his old friends he had been a corner-stone of the parish. They were all shocked at the suddenness of his going, saying, "But I saw him earlier this week out the road walking."

Soon there was no more time for talking and we all knelt and said the final rosary. Over the past few days, we had said the rosary many times and there is something extremely calming about its repetitive mantra. It is a family and community prayer, and in times of trauma, because it is a shared prayer, it encompasses all in a sense of togetherness.

When the rosary ended, the people eased out, and we as a family were left on our own to say our goodbyes. How do you say goodbye to forty-four years of loving and togetherness? Your insides disintegrate and, when the coffin lid goes down, you know that the best of your life is under it. My heart bled for Lena and the lads because Gabriel was the one who had loved them most in life.

Mike and Seán brought the coffin out the door and then the four of them shouldered their father past our home to the corner of the street. There, members of the Valley Rovers hurling and football club lined up and carried Gabriel up the hill. Since childhood he had been involved in the club and over the years had been chairman, secretary, treasurer and trainer; there had been times when I had thought the Valley Rovers were shooting balls through our house. People lined along both sides of the hill and, as the lighted church came into sight, the bell tolled.

A strange tranquillity descended on me. This was the place where Gabriel had spent so much time changing bulbs, brushing out leaves and blocking draughts. In some way, this was his place and he was coming home. It was the home of his spiritual side, which was a big part of Gabriel's life. So, up into the beautifully restored church, into which he had put so much love and effort, we brought Gabriel, and after the prayers people filed up to sympathise.

The "sorry for your trouble" procedure is probably a very Irish concept and when it is heartfelt and genuine it brings great comfort, but if it is delivered mechanically, as a matter of routine, with a limp handshake and no feeling, it is meaningless. One young lad of about ten came at the end of the queue and went straight for Mike who was his team trainer. He put his arms wordlessly around Mike's neck, gave him a hug and went straight out the door. It was an expression of deep sympathy and affection.

Gabriel's funeral mass brought me comfort. By chance or otherwise, the candelabrum by the altar was full of lighting candles, and light has a indefinably uplifting effect. Fr Pat's amazing homily opened new doors in my mind, leading me into zones of new thought. He told us that Gabriel's spirit was now part of something far greater and beyond our understanding, but emphasised that "Gabriel is dead." In the celebration of the life Gabriel had had and the welcoming of a new beginning we needed always to face the reality of death and the need to mourn. It was comforting to hear some of the prayers in the language that Gabriel loved, and Seán, who had inherited his father's love of our native tongue, gave the reading in Irish. My niece Treasa's wonderful voice filled the church. The pathos of the Pie Jesu gripped me and connected in a powerful way with the last hours of Gabriel's life. It brought a realisation that the separation of the divine soul from the earthly body is a huge wrenching. It is beyond all human understanding. The piteous agony of the Pie Jesu captures the trauma of that deep suffering. It had been beyond understanding until then.

As the bell tolled, the coffin, escorted by members of his bridge club, was taken down to Uncle Jacky and Aunty Peg's grave; as Gabriel was lowered into the earth, I thought: *The next coffin in there will be mine*. When the grave was covered, Treasa sang Gabriel's favorite song, "Carrigdown". Because the lads had asked me, I said a few words about him. I tried to convey as best I could that, soon after coming to Innishannon, I realised that I had married with this man an entire parish. Gabriel had really believed that we live in the shelter of each other. Then Con Murphy, who had taken Gabriel to the North Mon on his first day there, gave a wonderful tribute in Irish and English.

We returned to an overflowing house where the wonderful "kitchen staff" had everything under control. It was a day of talk, crying and comforting, and if an observer had looked in the window it might have seemed like a big family get-together. But the heart of the family was gone and we had a long hard road ahead of us.

CHAPTER
EIGHTEEN

The Grief Road

Nothing prepares for the ferocity of grief. You have a hard, cold pain in your gut, and where your mind was is now a black hole. You walk and talk as if you are normal and you may appear to be, but inside you are carrying around waves of knifing pain. This is the world of bereavement, a prison of desolation without walls.

Bereavement takes you on a solitary journey. Death disturbs your deepest roots and catapults you bruised, broken and unprepared on that journey. The light that normally leads you on is gone and, in that dark pit, you flounder around and grasp at nothingness. There is no escape. No easy way out. No short cut. Hurting encompasses like a shroud and grief takes hold and cripples.

Death is a cold, bleak subject. Even the very word strikes a chill into the mind. Is that why we sometimes avoid using it and prefer instead "passed away" or "gone to rest". But no matter what handle we put on it, death cannot be clothed in a flowery language that masks its face and makes it in any way easier to handle. For most of our life we may try to ignore it, like people walking backwards towards a cliff edge. But one day, when a loved one goes over that edge, we are forced to turn around and look death in the face.

Nothing prepares for the finality of death. Someone who was part of your life has gone and taken a chunk of you with them. The vacuum left by that chunk is a raw, bleeding hole. Death, as well as taking your loved one, has also taken part of you. You are left with a gaping wound. Grief is physical as well as mental. You have had a beloved limb amputated. But the bewildering thing is that your loved one is still part of your everyday thought pattern, and their presence is still around the house. You are living in two worlds — the before and after worlds. These two worlds are not welded together, so the ground beneath your feet is split with a deep chasm.

Into that deep hole people will throw thousands of words. If it was a sudden death, they will tell you, "At least he did not suffer." If it came after a long illness, you will be told, "Wasn't it a blessed relief?" And there is the sympathiser who will tell you of a far greater tragedy. As if that should make you feel better! They think by making you feel worse that you should feel better! They have no idea that bereavement is a frozen coat of mail, inside which you and all your mental anguish are completely trapped. Your pain is so intense that you have no space left into which other feelings can creep.

Friends may try to reason you out of your grief. But reason and grief have no relationship. Grief is raw emotion; reason does not come into it. When someone you love dies, deep dormant feelings escape out of a previously unquarried reservoir. Like a roaring tide let loose, they break down all barriers and sweep on, creating mental chaos. Grief has no respect for boundaries. It sweeps all before it. You are flattened and torn along in a ferocious flood, being belted off rocks of raw pain and crashed into deeper black holes. As you search for ease, you may come on a reading that tells you, "Death is nothing at all . . ." Then you might well think that you are losing your mind.

Previous death experiences reawaken; their healed scab is blown off and they add their old pain to the new. Ground that you had previously thought was firm beneath your feet shifts; you become a cauldron of doubt and terror. Where is the beginning and end of anything? You wake up in the morning and for one second you think that the nightmare has not happened. But then reality crashes in. Your mind is a whirl of black cloud; your legs are rigid with some kind of restraint that you cannot even begin to describe. It is as if there are iron rods where previously you had bone and muscle; as if where your stomach was is now a revolving churn. Black shadows and monsters awake with you and begin to slither around your mind. Another day begins!

Your grief is now, but past griefs also swim underneath. If as a child you lost a sibling or carry an unmourned death, that old trauma now stirs like a monster in an underground cave. He rises, and all past griefs become part of the present eruption.

You look around at people who have survived terrible trauma and you think, "How can they keep going?" I said this to a young widowed friend of mine and she smiled sadly and told me, "No choice." When I asked a friend, "Will I get over this?" she said wisely, "You will, because if people did not recover from grief, the world would come to a standstill."

Nevertheless, in grief your world certainly is at a standstill. It is impossible to reach over the void that separates you from the rest of the world. You are on an isolated island and the world is moving around outside but you have no wish to be part of it. You are cold and miserable and rendered immobile by hurt. All your energy is sapped by your grief so you are unable to distract yourself with activity. You feel like a bird whose wings have been brutally hacked off at the knuckle.

It is a time when prayer should help. But it may not do so. Your loved one has gone across that great divide into a place where all your prayers have gone. But heaven may be silent now and God may have become the God of no explanations. Your world here has been turned upside down, so how can you be comforted by a remote world? But in the dark of night, when a fierce storm rages, the deep roots of a tree hold it in the earth and the human spirit finds within it the power of amazing endurance.

As you struggle on, tiny stepping stones appear in front of you. They will be created by kindness, nature and your own inner resources, and by a source above and beyond our human understanding.

Cold Dawn

Grey light seeps in
And the razor edge
Of realisation cuts
Through my waking mind
The coldness of aloneness
Chills my nakedness.
Have I the courage
To reinvent myself
Because I was part
Of a whole?

Wet Blanket

My first day out
After the funeral
A stranger takes my hand,
"Sorry about your husband;
Buried mine ten years ago
Want you to know
It doesn't get any better."
Are the bereaved a coat hanger
For tales of misery?

The Gap

We went there together
But now I go alone
And cannot fill the space.
I want to go home
To lock myself in
Where I do not have
To hold back tears
And pretend to be normal.

Keeping Busy

Am I afraid to stop
In case all my pieces
Will fall apart
Could I disintegrate
And never come back
Together again?

The Backyard

With a mind full of throbbing pain
I washed the backyard
Each corner a thorn of memory.
Scalding tears joined piped water
Through hoses that you had joined.
When all was clean and rearranged
I asked myself, "Why did I bother?"
It is in the ordinary everyday
That I miss you most.
Savage grief must
Be worked through
And grappled with hour by hour
So that one day your memory
Could be a yard full of glowing flowers.

Climbing

With grim determination
I claw up the black face of grief
Gripping each ledge
Seeking tiny footholds
Because if I slip
I fall into nothingness
But if I keep climbing
You will be there
In the sunshine
Of wholeness.

Secrets

You are gone
Now I walk
The beach alone.
Pick up a black stone
Glistening with sea and sand,
Massage it in my palm.
The smooth hard stone
Enclosed and impenetrable
Is as incomprehensible
As death.

The Glen Falls

The roaring waterfall blew the crust
Off the hard wound of grief.
Screaming pain burst forth
Into the raging torrents.
Determined water penetrated
The depths of locked-up grief.
I cried with anger and relief
As foaming water washed out
Locked-up pain.
When the storm abated
I was more at home
With my deep sorrow
Cleansed in my inner being
Where icy water had
Penetrated the depths.

The Grief Road

On a cold January day
She visited
Exuding warmth and comfort.
She told me gently
"The sun will shine again."
On that frozen day
As we sat by a warm fire
She melted for a little while
My inner ice.
She was a constant caller
And walked with me
Along the road of grief.
She had been there
And knew the way
A friend who had learned
How to be a friend.

CHAPTER
NINETEEN

In the Shelter of
Each Other

"What are you doing on Dad's anniversary?" Diarmuid asked as the date of Gabriel's first anniversary loomed on the horizon.

"I'm trying not to think about it," I told him bleakly; "but the mass that morning will be for Gabriel. I've arranged it with Fr Kingston."

"And after that?" Diarmuid asked.

"Well, I suppose we'll all come down here for breakfast," I said.

"And then?" Diarmuid persisted.

"I've no idea," I told him wearily. I really did not want to think about it because every day was tough but the anniversary loomed before me like a tall, black cliff.

"I've an idea, but I'm not sure what you'll think about it," Diarmuid began tentatively.

"What is it?" I asked cautiously, in case I'd be letting myself in for something that I could not handle.

"You remember when we were all small, some Sundays we'd go to West Cork for picnics. I was thinking that, on Dad's anniversary, you and I and any of the others who want to could do the Ring of Beara. Dad loved that drive and at least we would all be together. What do you think?"

"Maybe it's not a bad idea," I agreed slowly. "It would be better than all being miserable in different corners."

"Say it to the rest of them anyway," he told me.

During the weeks before the anniversary, the happenings of the previous year replayed like a tape in my head. I wished that I could press the stop button or the fast forward, but on the grief road there is no stop button or fast forward. I was very grateful to our friends and neighbours who popped in or rang, and some brought garden plants or pot plants. Some plants went into the garden and some on Gabriel's grave. I had found throughout the year that visiting the grave had brought inexplicable comfort, and afterwards I would go in and sit in the quiet of the church where meditation quietened my chaotic mind. One evening, a neighbour whose wife had been killed in a road accident came into the church. As a teenager, his wife had worked during her holidays with us in the guesthouse, and Gabriel and herself had been good friends. Now we were both too upset for words, but words were not necessary because we were travellers on the same road.

One night when I came in home after locking up the ducks, there was a hank of beautiful wool and a pattern for a pair of socks on the kitchen table, with a note from a friend who was into knitting. I was delighted to get it and ran my fingers along the silky soft wool and studied the pattern. I am not a knitter, but the previous year when I was too distraught to read or watch television I had got the idea that I would like to knit, which came as a bit of a surprise because I had not knitted for years. So I got needles and sat by the fire in the *seomra ciúin* and knitted a simple scarf, and I found the soothing rhythm of knitting comforting. In recent days again I had thought of knitting and the idea of making a pair of socks had come into my mind. It was a strange coincidence that here on the table was the wool and the pattern.

That night, Lena held the hank of wool between her wrists and I wound it into a large, soft ball, something that I had not done since I was a child. So, knitting the sock began, and once again the warm fire and the knitting eased me on through raw days. A close friend who is a farmer and a few years previously had walked the grief road had told me that the first thing she did every morning after milking the cows was to light the fire. "In some way," she told me, "the fire was a comforter, and then when the summer came I stayed working in the garden every night until it was dark." I did as she had told me and found out that she was right.

In bereavement, you need every crutch that you can grasp. One of my crutches was the support of my kind friends and neighbours. In grief, your family is grieving too and trying to cope the best way they know how, and they are able to cope with only their own sorrow. So you need the neighbours. Some wise person once said, "It takes a village to rear a child." The same applies at

181

the other end of life. You grieve as part of the community to which your loved one belonged. Gabriel had been part of our parish and now it was helping me to cope. The Blasket Island people were right: "We live in the shelter of each other."

On the day before his anniversary, I planted a beech tree on the hill at the Kinsale end of the village. By choice I was on my own because the actual digging of the hole and the easing in of the tree and the shovelling of the earth around the young roots connected me in some indefinable way with Gabriel, and made me feel better. He had planted many trees around the village, including the lovely weeping willow at the foot of the Rock, and a few weeks before he died we had planted a companion for that tree by the grotto stream. There is an age-span of about thirty years between those two trees but in the life of a tree that span is soon eroded. The day after his funeral, we had planted an oak in the grotto and on the first day of the new year another oak in the church grounds. Eileen and Paddy, who are part of our extended family, had planted an oak on their farm in Farnagow, and Gabriel's friends, Jim and Antoinette, had selected a golden ash for the western end of the village near the Valley Rovers playing field. A golden ash is a lovely tree, and its association with the hurley made it the ideal choice. That Christmas I had given each of our children a tree to plant in memory of their father.

On the morning of the anniversary, Fr John, who had been a friend of Gabriel's, said the mass and that made things easier, and afterwards we walked across to the grave which was glowing with flowers; there we lit an outdoor candle as we had done on Christmas night. There is something especially comforting about a glowing candle in a sea of flowers.

After breakfast, we drove out into the depths of West Cork. It was a bright clear day; the majestic Beara Peninsula was wild, and its effect on my spirits was restoring. On the road to Allihies, a Buddhist temple has been built into the rock face, and when you sit there the sea stretches out in front of you and its immensity calms your soul. Down the road an ancient ruined lakeside castle was being rebuilt into a five-star luxury hotel, and further on was a tiny wayside church where Gabriel and I had once attended mass. We now visited and afterwards leaned over a stone wall, absorbing the beauty of the valley that sloped down into the crashing waves below.

On a visit to Kenmare a few years previously, Gabriel and I had enjoyed afternoon tea in the Sheen Falls Hotel, and besides the great food and the ceremony the staff made of the event, the view over the cascading waterfall and wood was what had really made this a memorable occasion. When we reached the hotel now, it was dusk, and the glowing fire welcomed us in; as we gathered around the table overlooking the waterfall, I came to the conclusion that Gabriel had been with us on our tour around the Beara Pensinula.

The days after the anniversary were hard, raw days, and I dreaded Christmas, but then something strange happened. One night I was alone in the house and decided to put up the crib. The crib has always held a

183

special place in my heart; ours is a collection of Aunty Peg's old crib figures and some of my own that the children had played with over the years, so now I had headless wise men and lame shepherds.

I have a belief that the original crib that humanity rejected was welcomed by the wild world, and over the years I have collected sheep, donkeys, cows and various other little animals and colourful birds. The result has been a menagerie of wild life. That night, I drew in the old bog deal and greenery from the garden and built the stable. When the stable was built, the lights would have to go in before the straw, the holy family and the rest of the entourage. Gabriel had always done the lighting but now I was on my own and clueless, but to my amazement every connection worked and the lights came on effortlessly. As the crib was laid out in the quietness of the empty house, a deep peace filled my heart and I felt a blanket of comfort enfold me. The hard lump of grief eased and Christmas was no longer a problem.

After Christmas, Diarmuid's thoughts turned to his forthcoming wedding and he asked me to write something suitable for their invitation card. I thought about it and decided that rather than write something new, I would share with them something that I had written for Gabriel many years previously.

Togetherness
Kept apart by busy days
We who belong together
As the interlaced fingers

Of praying hands
Come again at quiet times
At peace in our togetherness.

That poem was written after a stolen weekend. At the time, Gabriel and I were bogged down with a busy shop, a guesthouse and five children. Our bank manager was not a happy man because those were the days when they loved black bank balances, and we always seemed to be building and extending, driving up our overdraft to what he considered a dangerously high level. There were times when I thought that we would never get our heads above financial water. I was in charge of accounts, and each night as I counted the tills and checked the books I ate a giant Mars bar. It was my cigarette, my glass of brandy, my tranquiliser, my soother, and it should have turned me into a large fat lady, but because I was rushed off my feet, feeding children, checking deliveries and stocking shelves, it did not happen.

Life was so hectic that we sometimes forgot each other's birthdays, and one year it was a week after the date when we remembered our wedding anniversary. It was a time when I thought that it would be a great luxury to be able to stay in bed when I was sick. But that had not been possible as all the balls had to be kept in the air. On one of her visits, my mother, who was calmly stirring a tapioca pudding on the Aga, said to me: "Alice, of all my children, you were the one least likely to end up with such a busy life."

One of my less tactful sisters was more direct: "Well, there is no doubt about it," she told me emphatically, "that until you got married you were pure useless. You dodged every job when we were all growing up together at home. You were always up in the black loft, reading books. Gabriel made a great job out of you!"

Aren't sisters wonderful? Who else could be so brutally honest and get away with it? But whether she was right or not, we certainly had a busy schedule. There was no time or money for holidays and the only break was the All-Ireland Finals, to which we went with different children in tow.

I had cherished a hidden hope. It was that one weekend the two of us would steal away without chick or child and stay somewhere wonderful, pretending that we had no children, no dogs, no shop, no guests, no meetings. No one in the world only us! And the dream became a reality, because one warm, sunny Saturday in June we sat into the car and drove down to Kerry. When time is short, there is no time to waste on long travel and we had only until Sunday night. I think that God decided we deserved a break because it was a heavenly weekend. We had booked into the Parknasilla Hotel in Sneem, and, on the drive down, the heavy armour of work and responsibility slid off us as the Kerry mountains threw a warm blanket of relaxation around us. Our hotel room was up in an attic — if there is such a place in these hotels — and when we looked out of the window, we felt that we were sitting on top of the world.

186

We spent the day wandering around the woods that surrounded the hotel and when we reached the sea, we sat on a rock and chatted. It was great! No shop bell, no phones, no problems! That night we drove over to the Park Hotel in Kenmare and because everything was meant to go right, it did. We got a window table overlooking the river and, as we ate the moon came up across the water, which reflected the blues and purples of the surrounding mountains. It was a magical night and I remember thinking that it was great to be so happy.

The following morning, we had breakfast in bed. A pair of waiters arrived, bearing two silver trays laden with cooked breakfasts surrounded by exotic fruits and juices and sending out the whiff of fresh toast. This was breakfast in bed in style — this was luxury! Afterwards we walked along by the sea, and all that day we meandered around Kerry. We even bought an oil painting from a roadside artist. The bank manager was going to be yelling, but tomorrow was another day. That night, after we had come home, I wrote "Togetherness".

Now it was time to pass it on to the next generation.

CHAPTER
TWENTY

The Oldest Swinger
in Town

"Wouldn't it be lovely to have a dog again?" Lena suggested. "I loved Lady and Bran."

"They were great," I agreed.

"Your favourite was Captain," she said.

"He was indeed," I agreed. "I loved Captain."

An elegant black Doberman with the brains of Einstein and the bodywork of Naomi Campbell, Captain was so smart he could almost figure out what you were thinking. But he had one big weakness: he loved Flakes, those crumbly chocolate bars in yellow wrappers. He would sit in wait behind the back door of our shop, and when one of the staff unwittingly left it ajar he would nose in quietly. Then, fast as black lightning, he would sneak straight up to the chocolate stand, very delicately picking up a Flake and vanishing out the back door in a flash. Then he would go up into the garden where he would hide behind a shrub and open the wrapper so expertly that he did not even tear the paper. There he would chew away happily, and later the wrapper would tell its story.

188

One day on going into the shop, I met a startled customer, looking down the shopping aisle with a confused expression on her face.

"I'm not sure if this actually happened or did I have a hallucination," she told me in amazement. "Could a big black Doberman have darted in here and whipped a bar of chocolate?"

I assured her that she was not hallucinating. If it happened today, I might probably tell her that she was, because "health and safety" would close us down if they heard of such an occurrence.

Captain was king of the backyard; all the delivery men treated him with great respect and kept him at a safe distance. But Captain considered himself a superior animal and would not contaminate his jaws by biting a mere mortal. He was a gentleman and we all loved him. But one day he got very sick and Gearóid took him to the vet who thought that he had parvovirus and referred him to a vet in West Cork who was an expert on the disease. Despite all efforts, Captain died. He was buried in the grove with all the other dogs and cats who down through the years had passed through the house.

Hughie, who collected waste from the shop for his harriers, told me one day: "My collie bitch is in pup and when the pups are hardy, I'll bring you down two." On a cold January evening, the pups arrived, two absolutely adorable balls of black and white fur. We christened them Lady and Bran.

Lena was two at the time and an instant love affair burst into full bloom. They grew up with her, and wherever she went, they went — sometimes upstairs, where she hid them under her bed. Lady was a light-boned little bitch with a small, pointed, intelligent face, while Bran was a much bigger and stronger male but not as clever. They were inseparable and worked as a team, Lady constantly on red alert and Bran the solid back-up. When they became sexually active, steps had to be taken and, on the advice of Jim the vet, we took them to the veterinary clinic to have them neutered. After an examination, the vet on duty said to me, "Now, when these two are done, she will be the same dog but he will put on weight and become far less active, so maybe we might let him."

As I drove home with Bran relaxing on the back seat and my poor Lady behind in the clinic, waiting for her operation, I looked back at Bran and told him, "It's a man's world."

Later there were times when I regretted not having had Bran neutered because trying to keep him under restraint when a bewitching bitch was sending out signals of compliance was often a tug of war between two bitches. Philip, who lived in Bóthar na Sop and was the owner of a gorgeous Labrador that was any dog's fancy, would ring up and patiently inform me: "Bran is here again." Then I had to run over and drag the ardent lover, jumping with hormones, reluctantly home. Eventually we erected a wire fence along the penetrable part of the garden boundary, and that curtailed his ardour.

Within the fence, however, another problem raised its muddy head. Lady was a rooter, and any plant that went into the ground by day, she decided to uproot that night. As well as that, she slept in a different tub of flowers each night. She was a very clever dog and I could never understand why I could not get it into her brain cells that this was unacceptable behaviour. My father had an old saying: "O man of learning, thou art wrong, for instinct is more than wisdom strong." It certainly applied in Lady's case. When I decided to bark mulch all the flower beds, my gardening neighbour advised covering the earth beneath it with layers of old newspapers to improve its effectiveness. It sounded like a good idea but I discovered that we had two dogs who loved their morning papers. Before breakfast each day, the lawn was covered with discarded shredded newspapers. Gardening with Lady and Bran was a constant battle of wits — which they usually won.

They had one big terror in life, which they never overcame: thunder and lightning scared them senseless. When a thunderstorm came, they went berserk and sometimes ended up in the press under the stairs, and once when we were out during a thunderstorm, Lady took up residence inside the counter of the pub next door. In the end, a thunderstorm was Bran's undoing because one summer's night they were out in the garden when a sudden storm broke; Bran disappeared and we never again saw him. In his terror, he must have cleared the wall, and, despite intensive searches around the parish and ads in the local paper and on radio, we never found him. In his flight he could have run under a car or truck because it was as if he had disappeared into

191

thin air. For months afterwards whenever I saw a dog with his colouring I had a second look in case it was Bran. But we never again saw or heard of him.

Lady pined after him and never again went into the doghouse they had shared. When she died later, she too was buried in the grove at the top of the garden. I wrapped her in one of Lena's long-abandoned baby blankets and put a little headstone over her; that evening, when Lena came home from school, I had to tell her, and we both cried. But then Lena announced, "I never saw you crying since Nana died."

"Well, Nana wouldn't think much of that," I assured her, and we both laughed through our tears.

Lady and Bran had been with us for about fifteen years. Lady was my last burial in the grove and I sometimes smile to imagine that if on the last day a resurrection of animals takes place, there will be a big uprising at the top of our garden and a large army of dogs and cats will march out of the grove. Then we will find out what happened to Bran, because surely he will be reunited with his best friend Lady, and Lena will finally know the answer to her dilemma — "Did Bran go to heaven?" — because after he disappeared, when any friend or neighbour died, her first question was, "I wonder did they meet Bran?"

For many years after Lady and Bran, we remained without a dog. Lena and the boys had left home and I had turned into a gardener; the thought of a dog rampaging through Gabriel's green lawns and uprooting my plants, not to mention flattening my flower tubs, was more than I could entertain. On her regular holidays home, Lena sometimes said plaintively, "I miss the dogs", and one son would occasionally comment: "'Tis hard to get used to this place without a dog."

When Lena returned home, the talk of a dog resurfaced and I began to think that it might not be such a bad idea. It would have to be a smart dog, I thought, and the concept of a collie or a Doberman began to blossom in my head. We had loved Captain and the thought of another Captain appealed to me, but Lady and Bran had been great as well, so I dithered around with no final decision on the breed. We visited dogs' homes in Clonakilty and Cork, but a dogs' home is the wrong place for a ditherer, and I came home more confused than ever and decided to forget about the whole idea. Then the thought would resurface and I would look up the dog pages in the *Evening Echo;* I even made a few phone calls about Doberman pups but never quite got around to deciding anything.

Then fate stepped in: one morning at breakfast, Mike asked, "Have you given up on the dog craic?" and with my usual clarity of perception I replied, "Not sure I have or I haven't. Saw nothing that hit the spot in the dogs' homes or the paper. I think that I'll forget about it."

"Ever think of checking out *Buy and Sell?*" he asked.

"*Buy and Sell?*" I said in amazement. "Do they do dogs?"

"They do everything," he told me.

"I'll bring one in out of the shop," I decided and did just that. I went through it and found the dog pages, and there was an ad for two Dobermans, a year and a year-and-a-half old, with a telephone number for contact.

Before I could get second thoughts, I rang the number and a very polite English voice answered. When I asked about the dogs, he said that the family was emigrating and wanted a good home for them. I explained that we were an all-female household and wanted manageable dogs. He replied that that was exactly what he was looking for: he would prefer a female owner and did not want his dogs to be used solely as guard dogs as they had been reared as part of the family. Also he wanted them to go as a pair because they were used to being together. I told him that I'd ring him back and then sat down and had a cup of tea. What would I do? Instead of one dog, we could finish up with two. I had another cup of tea and then I rang Gearóid and told him my story.

"Where are they?" he asked.

"Waterford," I told him.

"I'll be down to you in ten minutes," he said.

I made a quick phone call to Lena, who was speechless with delight at the prospect of not one, but two, dogs. But I was not so sure.

It was a lovely May day and it took about two hours to get to Waterford; we followed directions and arrived at a beautiful lakeside house with a shining black Porsche parked outside.

"These dogs are going to move down the social ladder if they come home with us," Gearóid decided.

As we edged it open, we saw that a "Beware the dogs" sign was posted uninvitingly on the front gate.

"Guard dogs on duty" was on a black door to our right that I assumed accessed the garden. Again on the front door: "Guard dogs on duty". These dogs were certainly making their presence felt.

I swallowed hard as we waited for the front door to open. A dapper young Englishman invited us in and led us along a wide corridor into an impressive, ornately furnished room. The Dobermans had a lot on their plate. We had a few minutes of polite conversation and then the owner decided to let in the dogs so he left the room and a few minutes later two streaks of black lightning tore in the door. They circled the room a few times and then each one leapt on to a separate leather couch and viewed us with great suspicion. They were big, beautiful and intimidating.

We spent about two hours getting to know each other and, by the end of it, I knew that these two smart dogs sensed that we were up to no good. Their names were Kate and Lolly and they were two classy ladies — the fact that Kate's full title was Queen Kate came as no surprise. Even though I was a bit apprehensive of the undertaking, I had a feeling that they would probably come home with us. Their owner produced their papers, and their lineage was impeccable, with blue blood flowing through every vein in their bodies. They were virginal, untouched and immaculate.

Eventually the time came to make a move and the owner put their blanket on the back seat of our car and the two dogs jumped in on top of it. They were obviously accustomed to this procedure. He gave me a training video and a Doberman manual and a box full

195

of medical details and papers. I slipped into the back of the car, past the smaller of the two — which was Lolly — and sat between them; then we were on our way.

Sitting up on their haunches on either side, they towered over me like two black pillars. If they felt like a feed of Pedigree Chum, I was a sitting duck. After a few miles, Lolly decided to sit down and relax but Kate sat upright in frozen apprehension. Soon afterwards, she covered me and the seat in smelly vomit, and because we were in traffic Gearóid had to keep moving, so we were in a bit of a stinking puddle on the back seat. Further out the road, we were able to pull in and do a bit of a clean-up, always conscious of the fact that these two ladies — if given half a chance — could make a dash for freedom.

We finally arrived home with two very nervous dogs and one very apprehensive new owner. Gearóid drove into the backyard and shut the gate before releasing them from the car. They darted around, full of nervous apprehension, and then Queen Kate shot in the back door and, in very un-regal fashion, promptly deposited a huge pooh on the cream carpet in the front room.

Oh my God, I thought, *what am I after letting myself in for?*

"Don't mind that; it's just nerves," Gearóid assured me, and then, to my horror, added: "I hope that she's not marking her spot."

My misgivings about this new enterprise were growing by the minute. But when Lena came home an hour later, she had no such reservations and greeted them with whoops of joy, to which Lolly responded

196

with open-hearted abandon, while Queen Kate stood apart in an attitude of regal disdain. She was going to be a harder nut to crack, despite her queenly deposit on my cream carpet. When, in conversation on the phone with the now ex-owner, I told him that Kate was not settling in as well as Lolly, he assured me, "It will take Kate a while to settle. She's a one-owner dog whereas Lolly loves everyone. When Kate has sized everything up, she'll then decide to whom she will give allegiance."

So we would have to await queenly approval from Kate and see on whom she would confer her royal patronage!

We decided that they could lie on the rug-covered couch in the kitchen but would not have access to the couch and armchairs in the front room. So, after dinner, when we moved into that room, I draped myself along the couch and Lena and Ellen took over the two chairs; the dogs looked at us in disbelief and patrolled the room. These ladies were accustomed to royal treatment. Then it dawned on me that maybe they sat only on blankets and, when I laid one on the floor, they promptly took up residence. However, when Ellen leaned forward on her chair to explain something to Lena, Lolly immediately shot into the empty space behind her. But by the end of the evening, they had got the message.

That night, they slept on the couch in the kitchen and I got up during the small hours to check that all was in order. It was like being back on baby night-feeds. Their previous owner had instructed us that in the morning they were to be put on the lead and

197

taken to a specific place in the garden and told "Toilet". But either I did not have the right accent or they were just challenging my new role; so, when after half an hour nothing had happened, I decided that there had to be an easier way and left them off. They hit the garden like a hurricane and, having done a few laps of the lawn and knocked down a little stone man, they tore up into the grove and decided that this was the place for their private ceremony. That was the big issue decided, but the water outlet proved to have a more long-term effect because within weeks my lawn took on the appearance of Joseph's Technicolor coat.

Gradually they settled in and a routine developed. At night, they slept on the kitchen couch with the door open, so they had the run of the hallways, and one night when Lena forgot her key she found out that they were not very hospitable to strangers in the night. During the day, they had the run of the yard and garden but were tied up while deliveries were coming through the yard to the shop. Customers passing the open gate viewed them with surprise and felt happier that they were at a safe distance.

Kate and Lolly had a huge curiosity about their new surroundings and soon discovered that the big store to the back of our shop had a flat roof which then led them on to the flat roof of the pub next door. Part of the pub roof was glass, and they loved to go up there and watch the action below. One evening, an inebriated customer looked up to see two Dobermans looking down at him and promptly decided that he was not as sober as he had thought. After that, we had to bar them from pub visitations.

The neighbours called to see the "two girls" — as they were christened — and, once over the initial surprise at their size, everyone thought they were beautiful. Kate had decided that I was worthy of her patronage, or else she was smart enough to know that I was the source of the food, but in any case she followed me around like a shadow

All was going well until sex came into the picture. These were two well-bred bitches with royal connections, whose mothers and grandmothers had blue blood, and the fathers' contributions were also impeccable. They were not of the same litter but both had papers to impress. I had no interest in breeding or rearing litters of royal pups. I planned to get them neutered or spayed or fixed, though I did not even know the correct terminology. Gearóid, however, vehemently opposed this plan. We had head-on arguments with no solution. During these arguments, the word Nazi even came into play; I have been described as many things, but this was the first time that Hitler was invoked. So I decided to go underhand and booked them in with the vet without telling Gearóid, praying that he would not call during the recovery days. What he did not know would not bother him. Or so I thought.

When I visited the vet, I found a big shock waiting in the wings. She inspected the fasting dogs, and then told me that Kate was in heat. So I left Lolly, and an unhappy Kate came home and ran around the yard crying for Lolly. But she had more to cry about than missing Lolly. The previous week, there had been an incident that at the time had been of little consequence but in the light of Kate's condition could be nothing short of a canine disaster.

Around our village rambles a geriatric mongrel, Jack the Lad, himself the product of a long line of one-night stands. He could be a cross between a greyhound, a terrier, a sheepdog and a Labrador; his bloodline would confuse any DNA test. Over the years, when he ambled around the village, eyeing the local talent, it was a case of lock up your bitches. Now he could hardly walk but the big question was, how geriatric was Jack the Lad? Because the previous week, while the gate was open for deliveries, he had come into our yard and had gone up into the garden and hidden in the bushes until the gate was locked and the girls were let loose. An hour later, I had glanced out the window and there, to my horror, between my two beautiful girls was Jack the Lad. I nearly fainted! I shot out the back door and booted Jack the Lad out the gate with every intention of damaging his artillery. Now the burning question was, had he or had he not? I rang my sister Ellen, who had returned to Canada.

"Ah, Alice," she assured me, "Jack the Lad is too old; he couldn't rise to any occasion."

But how old was too old? I rang my friend Mary and explained my dilemma, adding, "But he wasn't in the yard very long."

"Long enough for Jack the Lad," she informed me.

I rang Paddy who, as a farmer, could be expected to know everything about sex in animals.

"Oh, there's a morning-after pill for cows now," he assured me cheerfully.

"Paddy, this morning after was five mornings ago," I told him apprehensively.

"Oh, Alice, you don't need a morning-after pill," he told me regretfully. "You need a miracle."

To add to my troubles, Gearóid called unexpectedly and, when I heard his voice out in the yard asking Kate where Lolly was, I felt like running for cover. But I had to face the music, and a raging son went in to the vet to collect Lolly, who arrived home in a prone state, much to Kate's consternation. But her consternation was nothing compared to mine. When I looked at my beautiful Kate and thought of the geriatric mongrel who could have polluted her well-bred elegance, I came out in a cold sweat.

The following day, after a veterinary consultation, I was told to bring Kate in the following Monday and he would do the needful. The days passed slowly and I watched Kate for signs of morning sickness but she was in fine fettle. Maybe dogs don't have morning sickness. I was so relieved when the day came and she went into the veterinary clinic; later that day, the vet informed me that all was well and that Jack the Lad could no longer pose a problem. But I wanted the answer to one question: had Jack the Lad invaded virgin territory or had he not? The answer was, he had.

That evening, I waited at my front door with murder in my heart and watched Jack the Lad drag himself down the street. He was fifteen years old, which in human terms is one hundred and five. Slowly easing forward his front right leg, he gradually pulled that half of his body along and then, gradually pushing forward his left leg, he painfully dragged his second half along. Very slowly he came down the street. He had to stop every few seconds to draw a laboured breath, and I could hear his lungs rattling from ten feet away. As I viewed him, I found it difficult to believe that there was life in that old dog yet. He certainly had to be the oldest swinger in town.

CHAPTER
TWENTY-ONE

A Challenge

"Great God!" Steve exclaimed in horror — which was a bit rich coming from this man who does not believe in divine existence. I was tempted to come out with Gabriel's response in similar circumstances. If Gabriel had given you a shock by suddenly coming unexpectedly around a corner and you reacted by gasping, "Oh, God!" Gabriel would smile and say, "No, I'm Gabriel." It was a family joke with which Steve would probably not have been impressed. Now I watched his reaction to my once-beautiful garden.

Steve, who is the editor at Brandon, had seen the garden for the first time twenty years earlier when he had come to take a photograph before my first book, *To School Through the Fields* was published. He had wandered around our overgrown, dog-friendly garden and was heard to mutter to himself, "Is there any corner here that resembles a garden?" In later years, when I caught the gardening bug, he had to eat his words, and one day he acidly informed me: "When I came here first, it was all about writing and no gardening, and now it's all gardening and no writing."

Now he stood at my garden gate and surveyed in disbelief what lay in front of him.

"What happened here?" he demanded, and the answer took just one word.

"Dogs," I said.

"Good God!" he declared in his best Anglo-Irish accent. Born into a posh Dublin background and educated in England, he came in later life to live and work in Dingle where, over the years, he turned into a lapsed Anglo-Irishman whose BBC accent succumbed to the soft *blás* of the Kerry mountains. His accent became that of an Anglo-Irish Kerryman, but on certain occasions, when under emotional stress, he reverted like some of my garden shrubs to the original of the species.

"What are you going to do now?" he asked with searching precision, and again it took just one word.

"Redesign," I told him.

All my adult life, one of my gardening neighbours had constantly assured me that dogs and gardening did not a successful marriage make. Now was the time to prove her wrong; to try to effect a compromise acceptable to all parties. There were three of us in this marriage bed: the dogs, the garden and me. The dogs were the dominant party, the garden the sleeping partner and I was the liaison officer trying to make the whole thing work. A divorce had to be avoided at all costs. I knew that I had a big job on my hands but the stakes were high. I loved my garden and had grown to love my dogs, and I wanted all to live in peace.

Peace is not a word that two exuberant Dobermans bring to mind. In their lineage are greyhound genes, and they proved it by turning my garden into Shelbourne Park. In front of the gate was a wide lawn with a sweeping curve around an old apple tree, and Kate and Lolly would round this turn at breakneck speed. As I watched them, a Grand National radio commentary from my childhood would come to mind and I would recall the voice of Peter O'Sullivan: "And now they are coming up to the canal turn." When this was taking place, tufts of grass would scatter in their wake and then they would slam on the brakes, leaving skid marks across the lawn.

After a while, my lawn became a thing of the past. This did not happen overnight: the dogs came in May, which was a good month because the lawns were dry and firm and most of the shrubs were in their full health, but during the summer Kate and Lolly tested the well-being of the shrubs. Anything too fragile for their exuberance died underfoot. It was good that the garden was mature: most of the shrubs were able to contend with the constant assault; but as the fine weather faded, so did my lawn. Bitch urine and the Grand National on a daily basis proved more than any lawn could endure. A great Irishman once said, "Victory is won not by those who can inflict the most, but by those who can endure the most." My lawns could endure no more; it was time for a major rethink.

Gardens talk to you, so I walked around my garden and listened to it; we had long debates about possibilities and impossibilities. The list of the latter was

205

slightly longer than the list of the former, but there was no future in negative thinking. As I walked around, I constantly reminded myself that Uncle Jacky had gardened here with two dogs, three cats and about twenty hens. So what had I to complain about? I began gradually to work out a feasible plan. Then there came a sense of excitement at the concept of a whole new garden and a whole new challenge. This was going to test all my ingenuity and my limited gardening skills.

As I walked around, devising my plans, the two culprits accompanied me and when, in a fit of exuberance, they raised themselves on their hind legs and danced together on top of flowers or tore around the apple tree turn to test which of them might win the Gold Cup, they kept me aware of the necessity for basic solid structure. Neighbours who dropped in raised their eyes to heaven and one friend told me, "You're actually gardening for two dogs." He was right.

With a vague plan in mind, I strode around the garden in long strides to get measurements. Uncle Jacky had never used a measuring tape but had gauged the length of his stride and measured accordingly. It was a handy gardening ploy. That night I put the design on paper. It looked good, but then everything can look good on paper. On my showing it to a gardening neighbour, she gasped: "No lawn!" But no lawn was better than a yellow brick road or a winter sea of mud.

In Boston, when they were implementing a huge redesign of the entire city, it was christened the Big Dig; it went on for years. Starting out on my own Big Dig, I hoped it would be short term. As a one-digger outfit, I could work all the hours that God gave.

There is nothing more therapeutic than digging: we are deeply connected with the earth, and working with it soothes our inner being. When I began my Big Dig, I was deeply grieving the loss of Gabriel, and those long hours spent digging in the garden were better than tranquilisers or counselling. There is no way to explain this because it has to be experienced to understand the concept. It is as if in some way the bleeding wound of amputation that is death soaks down into the brown earth and the earth draws out the festering wound of grief. Then the earth becomes a poultice for the wound. All this happens while you are occupied doing something else. I was busy redoing the garden and the dogs were in heaven because I was with them every day.

I soon discovered that more than the appearance of the garden had changed. Prior to dogs, gardening gloves could be dropped and trowels left in every corner, and there they remained. Now Kate and Lolly had tugs of war with my gardening gloves, and my pruners developed chewed handles. The price of keeping things safe from them was eternal vigilance. I hid pruners up trees and promptly forgot where I had put them; I tucked gloves into the elbows of branches where they were discovered weeks later. When I confessed this to a neighbour who was keeping an eye on my progress, he told me, "You're a member of CRAFT", and when I asked what that meant, I was told: "Can't Remember A Fecking Thing." I certainly qualified for membership.

ongoing battle, but despite all the upheavals the garden is now beginning to take shape and develop a whole new look.

A garden, like life, is a constant challenge. In order to cope with the changing times, I had had to redesign my garden. I had been reluctant to start but the task proved to be both challenging and rewarding. Our parish, too, has been going through changing times. Much new planting and transplanting has gone on, and continues. But the old residents, like Uncle Jack's mature trees, provide the shelter-belt for the new planting. Those who occupy the apartments that have sprung up in the village are like bedding plants — probably most of them here on a short-term basis. Some new householders, like the freshly planted shrubs, may take a while to settle in and will have to invest energy in their new soil before they take root. Some old residents, like the mature shrubs, may be feeling a bit overcrowded and may have to prune back a little to give space to the new plantation. The farming community runs like a sheltering hedge through our parish and, if too much of our farmland disappears under concrete developments, the soul of rural Ireland will be damaged. The big question is: can we recreate a new supportive community within our changed landscape and extended boundaries? All in all, challenging times.

Behind the Scenes at the Museum of Baked Beans

Hunter Davies

Driven by his own passion for collecting, Hunter Davies has packed his notepad and set off in search of Britain's maddest museums. As he explores these hidden gems he soon discovers that they are everywhere and that they celebrate just about everything, from lawnmowers in Southport to pencils in Keswick.

But as Hunter travels up and down the country he comes to realise that it isn't only the collections that are fascinating, it's also the people who have put them together.

Whether they're a man who loves Heinz so much he's changed his name to Captain Beany or a kleptomaniac Vintage Radio buff, these eccentric collectors are Britain's finest and could live in no other country in the world. Once you discover these museums and get to know their curators, Great Britain won't look quite the same again . . .

ISBN 978-0-7531-5279-9 (hb)
ISBN 978-0-7531-5280-5 (pb)

House of Memories

Alice Taylor

House of Memories shows her in her prime as a novelist
                                                    Irish Independent

A story of love for the home and of the passions and jealousies it can inspire. Following his brutish father's unlamented death, young Danny Conway strives to rescue the family farm from ruin; when all seems hopeless, help comes from the most unexpected quarter.

House of Memories tells a story of resilience in the face of family tragedy; a story, too, of bereavement and grief, and of trying to cope with loss. No one knows the weft and warp of country life as Alice Taylor does, and in her third novel she again displays her unique ability to capture its rhythms and cadences.

ISBN 978-0-7531-7533-0 (hb)
ISBN 978-0-7531-7534-7 (pb)

The Village

Alice Taylor

By the author of To School Through the Fields

"Taylor has a knack for finding the universal truth in daily details." Los Angeles Times

"There is charm and humour in *The Village* as well as a quality perhaps best described as loving kindness." Irish Independent

"She has a wicked wit and a pen which works on the reader slowly but insidiously." Observer

As Alice Taylor put it:"This is the story of life in a village; it is the story, too, of a small shop and a post office . . . this is also the story of an ordinary young wife and mother who was sometimes bored by the monotonous everyday routine of housework and children, and who in an effort to make life more interesting became part of the changing village scene."

ISBN 978-0-7531-9964-0 (hb)
ISBN 978-0-7531-9967-1 (pb)

ISIS publish a wide range of books in large print, from fiction to biography. Any suggestions for books you would like to see in large print or audio are always welcome. Please send to the Editorial Department at:

ISIS Publishing Limited
7 Centremead
Osney Mead
Oxford OX2 0ES

A full list of titles is available free of charge from:

Ulverscroft Large Print Books Limited

(UK)
The Green
Bradgate Road, Anstey
Leicester LE7 7FU
Tel: (0116) 236 4325

(Australia)
P.O. Box 314
St Leonards
NSW 1590
Tel: (02) 9436 2622

(USA)
P.O. Box 1230
West Seneca
N.Y. 14224-1230
Tel: (716) 674 4270

(Canada)
P.O. Box 80038
Burlington
Ontario L7L 6B1
Tel: (905) 637 8734

(New Zealand)
P.O. Box 456
Feilding
Tel: (06) 323 6828

Details of **ISIS** complete and unabridged audio books are also available from these offices. Alternatively, contact your local library for details of their collection of **ISIS** large print and unabridged audio books.